The Faber Book of
EPIGRAMS AND EPITAPHS

the
Faber Book
of
Epigrams
&
Epitaphs

EDITED
WITH AN INTRODUCTION
BY

Geoffrey Grigson

Faber & Faber

LONDON · BOSTON

First published in 1977
by Faber and Faber Limited
3 Queen Square London WC1
Reprinted 1979
Printed in Great Britain by
Whitstable Litho Ltd Whitstable Kent
All rights reserved

BRITISH LIBRARY CATALOGUING
IN PUBLICATION DATA
Faber book of epigrams and epitaphs
1. Epigrams, English
I. Grigson, Geoffrey
821'.008   PR 1195.E/
ISBN 0-571-10990-X
ISBN 0-571-11090-8 Pbk

Contents

to MARY RAYNER

Introduction

SIR THOMAS BROWNE (who liked epigrams and epitaphs) wrote down in his commonplace book that the bones from the charnel house of St. Paul's—more than a thousand cartloads of them—were transported to Finsbury Fields, "and there layd in a moorish place, with so much soyle to cover them as raysed the ground for three windmills, which have since been built there".

It was a proper subject, he thought, for an epigram: "To make an epigramme or a fewe verses . . . of a windmill upon a mount of bones."

There you have one idea of what an epigram should be: sententious and pointed—grinding food for the living on the bones of the dead—and unexpected, yet applicable to our general experience.

Epigrams no doubt made Sir Thomas Browne think of the Roman epigrammatist Martial. All educated men of Browne's century (or the 16th century, or the 18th, or the 19th) were familiar with Martial's epigrams, witty, hard, brutal, and indecently brutal, many of them. They all knew that an epigram wasn't necessarily short, though it inclined that way. Martial had sometimes written two lines, sometimes twenty. They would have known that poems of a different character were also epigrams, tender and light poems from the *Greek Anthology*. They would have expected both kinds from an English (or French or Italian) poet of any consequence. If Sir Thomas Browne had picked up *Hesperides* by his contemporary Robert Herrick, which came out only ten years before his *Urne-Buriall*, he would have found both the derivatives from Martial (if rather crude and blunt in an unsuccessful way) and the derivatives from the gentler and subtler Greek epigrams; a mixture of what one Elizabethan writer (William Camden), in defining epigrams, described as "short and sweete poems, framed to praise or dispraise".

The fact is that since they began to write epigrams

(first of all in imitation of the Latinists of the Renaissance, who in turn had imitated Martial and the Greeks) most English poets have mixed epigrams of praise and dispraise, according to temperament and mood, and period. They have pleased themselves (and their readers) with being gnomic and witty and delicate and brutal and grotesque. They have written for fun, decently and indecently. What they haven't laid down is anything like a Japanese division into *haiku* and *senryu*. Both *haiku* and *senryu* are epigrams—if epigram is taken to mean brevity; but a *haiku* has been defined as expressing a moment of vision into the nature of the world and a *senryu* as expressing a moment of satirical insight into the nature of ourselves:

> The girl,
>   As he loves her up,
>   Talks only to the cat.

With us, rather unfortunately, "epigram" has come only to suggest something like *senryu*, short and sharp, with no better companion word for the epigram, like so many by Herrick, which is short and celebratory, the epigram which is tender instead of satirical, than "lyric", vaguely used. Still, here is a selection of both kinds, from six centuries.

Point, it can be claimed, is what distinguishes and unites epigrams—

> Epigrams must be curt, nor seem
> Tail-pieces to a poet's dream . . .

To be curt is to be pointed, "to the point"; and since poetry should always be to the point, as far as possible without superfluousness, that really is to say that a good epigram has simply to be a good poem. Like other poems it has to be a particular structure of general application.

Epigrams at the quite enjoyable level of ordinary manufacture—say by university or legal wits—incline to hop from rhyme to rhyme with little structure or substance in between. Epigram collections have usually been crowded with examples which are marked, between the rhymes, by, for one thing, an awkward unconvincing alteration of the usual order of sentences. Epigrams haven't room for interference or interruption of that kind. One of the earlier practitioners, Ben Jonson, who was rather heavy than rough, realized that many epigrams failed "because they expressed in the end what should have been understood by what was said", meaning, I think, that epigrams need to be *poem* all the way through, or congruous with their point all the way through, instead of working lamely to a revelation which comes only at the end. Sheridan's epigram about poor Queen Caroline's friend, Lady Anne Hamilton, (No. 347) seems a good example of what Jonson meant. All the way through it is a funny and economical take-off of ill-natured gossip, a good example of point distributed or extended.

Epigrams being poems in this way, obviously it is the poets who write them best—Herrick, Prior, Pope, Blake, Burns, Landor, Robert Graves, Stevie Smith, etc.— rather than the amateur, occasional word-spinners.

When he was writing about Kipling, T. S. Eliot maintained that good epigrams in English were very few. I am not so sure. But at any rate in putting this collection together I have aimed to welcome rather than raise objections or insist on distinctions. The epigram extends to the *jeu d'esprit*; and of course, but there will be no argument about that, it includes the epitaph. From antiquity and through European literature epitaphs have been "framed to praise or dispraise", the rubbings from the imaginary tomb, as if the original Greek *epigramma* had been abstracted from the monuments along the roadway. "Here lies", "Stop, traveller", "Tread softly", "Lie lightly, earth", all these conventions of the literary epitaph go back to the classical beginnings, in the *Greek Anthology*.

Perhaps Eliot's stricture should be amended to say that good epigrams, like other good poems, are few enough in any language. But then at any rate effective epigrams do afford an essence of what can be made with words. The effective poet is someone always in play with words; and for its writer each epigram solves a problem in words – how with economy and without circumlocution to make out of them something with force which seems unforced, and is also piquant and apt to life, and memorable.

Many of these short poems went so much from collection to collection and mouth to mouth that the names of those who wrote them – this happened particularly in the 16th and 17th centuries – were frequently rubbed off on the way. I would be grateful to be told of any names which should be re-affixed, on manuscript or printed authority, to epigrams printed here as anonymous, or to epigrams wrongly ascribed. Some of them run so well that they must have been made up – like some of the best bawdy but anonymous limericks of the last hundred years or so – by poets of ability and renown; and the parents should be restored to their children.

Geoffrey Grigson

THE EPIGRAMS AND EPITAPHS

EPITAPHY OF LA GRAUNDE AMOURE   1

> O mortall folke! you may beholde and se
> Howe I lye here, sometime a myghty knyght;
> The end of joye and all prosperite
> Is deth at last, through his course and myght;
> After the day there cometh the derke night;
> For though the day be never so longe,
> At last the belles ringeth to evensonge.
>
> And my selfe called La Graunde Amoure,
> Seking adventure in the worldly glory,
> For to attayne the riches and honour,
> Did thinke full lytle that I should here lye,
> Tyll deth dyde marke me full ryght pryvely.
> Lo what I am! and wherto you must!
> Lyke as I am so shall you be all dust.
>
> Than in your mynde inwardly despyse
> The bryttle worlde, so full of doublenes,
> With the vyle flesshe, and ryght sone aryse
> Out of your slepe of mortall hevynes;
> Subdue the devill with grace and mekenes,
> That after your lyfe frayle and transitory,
> You may than live in joy perdurably.

ANONYMOUS

TEN COMMANDMENTS, SEVEN   2
DEADLY SINS, AND FIVE WITS

> Kepe well x and flee fro vii;
> Rule well v and come to hevyn.

The earth goes on the earth glittering in gold,
The earth goes to the earth sooner than it wold;
The earth builds on the earth castles and towers,
The earth says to the earth, All this is ours.

JOHN HEYWOOD
1497?–1580?

4   OF BOTCHING

God is no botcher, but when God wrought you two,
God wrought as like a botcher, as God might do.

5   OF USE

Use maketh maistry, this hath been said alway:
But all is not alway: as all men do say,
In Aprill the Koocoo can sing her song by rote.
In June out of tune she can not sing a note.
At first, kooco, kooco, sing still can she do,
At last kooke, kooke, kooke: six kookes to one ko.

THE COURTIER'S LIFE   6

In court to serve decked with fresh array,
Of sugar'd meats feeling the sweet repast,
The life in banquets, and sundry kinds of play
Amid the press of lordly looks to waste
Hath with it join'd oft times such bitter taste,
  That who so joys such kinds of life to hold,
  In prison joys, fetter'd with chains of gold.

ANONYMOUS

ON THE EARL OF KILDARE   7

Who kill'd Kildare? Who dar'd Kildare to kill?
Death kill'd Kildare, who dare kill whom he will.

HENRY HOWARD, EARL OF SURREY
1517?–1547

THE MEANS TO ATTAIN HAPPY LIFE*   8

My friend, the things that do attain
  The happy life be these, I find:
The riches left, not got with pain;
  The fruitful ground, the quiet mind;

The equal friend; no grudge, no strife;
  No charge of rule, nor governance;
Without disease the healthy life;
  The household of continuance;

* For Ben Jonson's version, see No. 83.

The mean diet, no dainty fare;
  Wisdom joined with simpleness;
The night discharged of all care,
  Where wine the wit may not oppress;

The faithful wife, without debate;
  Such sleeps as may beguile the night:
Content thyself with thine estate,
  Neither wish death, nor fear his might.

(From the Latin of Martial)

9   EXHORTATION TO LEARN
BY OTHERS' TROUBLE

My Ratcliffe, when thy rechless youth offends,
Receive thy scourge by others' chastisement.
For such calling, when it works none amends,
Then plagues are sent without advertisement.
Yet Salomon said, the wronged shall recure:
But Wyatt said true, the scar doth aye endure.

GEORGE TURBERVILLE
c. 1540–c. 1598

10   OF ONE THAT HAD A GREAT NOSE

Stand with thy nose against
  the sun with open chaps,
And by thy teeth we shall discern
  what 'tis a clock, perhaps.

(From the Greek of the Emperor Trajan)

THE LOVER TO HIS LADY, THAT GAZED
MUCH UP TO THE SKIES

My girl, thou gazest much
 upon the golden skies:
Would I were Heaven! I would behold
 thee with all mine eyes.

(After the Greek of Plato)

AN EPITAPH OF MAISTER WIN
DROWNED IN THE SEA

Whoso thou art that passest by this place,
And run'st at random on the slipper way,
Recline thy list'ning ear to me a space,
Do stay thy ship and hearken what I say:
Cast anchor here until my tale be done,
So may'st thou chance the like mishap to shun.

Learn this of me, that men do live to die
And Death decays the worthiest wights of all;
No worldly wealth or kingdoms can supply
Or guard their princes from their fatal fall:
One way we come unto this life we see,
And to be rid thereof a thousand be.

My gallant youth and frolic years behight
Me longer age, and silver hairs to have;
I thought my day would never come to night,
My prime provok'd me to forget my grave:
I thought by water to have scap'd the death
That now amid the seas do lose my breath.

Now, now, the churlish channel me do chock,
Now surging seas conspire to breed my cark,
Now fighting floods enforce me to the rock,
Charybdis' whelps and Scylla's dogs do bark,
Now hope of life is past, now, now, I see
That W. can no more a livesman be.

Yet do I well affy for my dessart,
(When cruel death hath done the worst it may),
Of well-renowned fame to have a part
To save my name from ruin and decay:
And that is all that thou or I may gain,
And so adieu, I thank thee for thy pain.

EDWARD DE VERE, EARL OF OXFORD
1550–1604

13   EPIGRAM

Were I a king, I could command content;
    Were I obscure, hidden should be my cares;
Or were I dead, no cares should me torment,
    Nor hopes, nor hates, nor loves, nor griefs, nor fears.
        A doubtful choice, of these three which to crave,
        A kingdom, or a cottage, or a grave.

When wert thou born, Desire?
    In pride and pomp of May,
By whom, sweet boy, wert thou begot?
    By Self Conceit, men say.
Tell me, who was thy nurse?
    Fresh Youth, in sugar'd joy.
What was thy meat and daily food?
    Sad sighs and great annoy.
What haddest thou to drink?
    Unfeigned lovers' tears.
What cradle wert thou rocked in?
    In hope devoid of fears.
What brought thee to thy sleep?
    Sweet thoughts, which liked me best.
And where is now thy dwelling-place?
    In gentle hearts I rest.
Doth company displease?
    It doth, in many one.
Where would Desire then choose to be?
    He loves to muse alone.
What feedeth most thy sight?
    To gaze, on favour still.
Whom find'st thou most thy foe?
    Disdain of my good will.
Will ever age or death
    Bring thee unto decay?
No, no! Desire both lives and dies
    A thousand times a day.

(After the Latin of George Buchanan)

⟨HIS EPITAPH⟩
15   WHICH HE WRIT THE NIGHT BEFORE
HIS EXECUTION

Even such is time that takes in trust
Our youth, our joys, and all we have,
And pays us but with age and dust:
Who in the dark and silent grave
When we have wandred all our ways
Shuts up the story of our days.
And from which earth and grave and dust
The Lord shall raise me up, I trust.

16   ON THE SNUFF OF A CANDLE
THE NIGHT BEFORE HE DIED

Cowards fear to die, but Courage stout,
Rather than live in snuff, will be put out.

17   The sun may set and rise:
But we contrariwise
Sleep after our short light
One everlasting night.

(After the Latin of Catullus)

OF TREASON   18

Treason doth never prosper, what's the reason?
For if it prosper, none dare call it treason.

THE AUTHOR, OF HIS OWN FORTUNE   19

Take fortune as it falls, as one adviseth:
Yet Heywood bids me take it as it riseth,
And while I think to do as both do teach,
It falls and riseth quite beside my reach.

OF A FAIR SHREW   20

Fair, rich, and young? how rare is her perfection,
Were it not mingled with one foul infection.
I mean, so proud a heart, so curst a tongue,
As makes her seem, nor fair, nor rich, nor young.

AGAINST AN OLD LECHER   21

Since thy third curing of the French infection,
Priapus hath in thee found no erection,
Yet eat'st thou ringoes, and potato roots,
And caviar, but it little boots.
Besides the bed's head a bottle's lately found,
Of liquor that a quart cost twenty pound:
For shame, if not more grace, yet shew more wit,

Surcease, now sin leaves thee, to follow it.
Some smile, I sigh, to see thy madness such
That that which stands not, stands thee in so much.

22 OF A ZEALOUS LADY

Two aldermen, three lawyers, five physicians,
Seven captains, with nine poets, ten musicians,
Woo'd all one wench. She, weighing all conditions
By which she might attain to most promotion,
Did take a priest at last for pure devotion.

(*After the Latin of Martial*)

ANONYMOUS
23 Beneath this smooth stone by the bone of his bone
Sleeps Master John Gill;
By lies when alive this attorney did thrive,
And now that he's dead he lies still.

24 ON JOHN SO

So died John So.
So so, did he so?
So did he live,
And so did he die!
So so, did he so,
And so let him lie.

Here lies John Knott:
His father was Knott before him,
He lived Knott, died Knott,
Yet underneath this stone doth lie
Knott christened, Knott begot,
And here he lies and still is Knott.

JOSHUA SYLVESTER
1563–1618

OMNIA SOMNIA★   26

Go, silly worm, drudge, trudge, and travel,
     Despising pain,
     So thou may'st gain
Some honour, or some golden gravel:
But Death the while (to fill his number)
     With sudden call
     Takes thee from all,
To prove thy days but dream and slumber.

FUIMUS FUMUS†   27

Where, where are now the great reports
Of those huge haughty earth-born giants?
    Where are the lofty tow'rs and forts
Of those proud kings bade Heav'n defiance?
    When them I to my mind revoke,
    Methinks I see a mighty smoke
Thick mounting from quick-burning matter
Which in an instant winds do scatter.

★ Everything is a dream.   † We were smoke.

⟨QUATRAIN⟩

When wine runs low, it is not worth the sparing;
The worst and least doth to the bottom dive:
Wrong not thy leisure, years vouchsafe, in daring:
But sometimes look into thy grave, alive.

(From the French of Pierre Mathieu)

29   ⟨QUATRAIN⟩

I hate these phrases: Of power absolute,
Of full authority, Full proper motion.
The divine laws they have trod under foot—
And human too—for private man's promotion.

(From the French of Guy du Faur de Pibrac)

30   *MUNDUS QUALIS★*

What is the world? tell, Worldling (if thou know it).
    If it be good, why do all ills o'erflow it?
If it be bad, why dost thou like it so?
    If it be sweet, how comes it bitter then?
    If it be bitter, what bewitcheth men?
If it be friend, why kills it (as a foe)
    Vain-minded men that over-love and lust it?
    If it be foe, Fondling, how dar'st thou trust it?

★ Such is the world.

The stranger, wond'ring, stalks, and stares upon
    Rome's antique glories, in her ruins seen;
He sees high arches, huge shining heaps of stone,
    Maim'd, mutil'd, murder'd, by years' wasteful teen:
He sees a rugged, ragged, rocky quarr
    Hang in the air, with ivy laced about.
O! what can last, alas! (then cries he out)
    Sith Time hath conquer'd the world's conqueror?

JOHN DAVIES OF HEREFORD
1565?–1618

AGAINST GAUDY-BRAGGING-UNDOUGHTY   32
DACCUS

Daccus is all bedaub'd with golden lace,
    Hose, doublet, jerkin; and gamashes too;
Yet is he foolish, rude, and beastly-base,
Crows like a cock, but like a craven does:
    Then he's (to prize him nought his worth beneath)
    A leaden rapier in a golden sheath.

OF KATE'S BALDNESS   33

By's beard the Goat, by his bush-tail the Fox,
By's paws the Lion, by his horns the Ox,
By these all these are known; and by her locks
That now are fall'n, Kate's known to have the pox.

Sith Venus had her mole, Helen her stain,
Cynthia her spots, the Swan hath sable feet,
The clearest day some cloud, the smoothest plain
Some hole, or hillock, why should Phryna fret
    When she is said to have a ruby nose,
    Sith that is rich, and all her rareness shows?

ANONYMOUS

35
    Here lie I, Martin Elginbrod.
    Hae mercy on my soul, Lord God;
    As I would do, were I Lord God,
    And ye were Martin Elginbrod.

36   ON THE EARL OF LEICESTER

    Here lieth the worthy warrior
      Who never bloodied sword;
    Here lieth the noble counsellor,
      Who never held his word.

    Here lieth his Excellency,
      Who ruled all the state;
    Here lieth the Earl of Leicester,
      Whom all the world did hate.

All Christian men in my behalf,
Pray for the soul of Sir John Calf.
O cruel death, as subtle as a fox,
Who would not let this calf live till he had been an ox,
That he might have eaten both brambles and thorns,
And when he came to his father's years might have worn horns.

A CASE TO THE CIVILIANS★   38

Nokes went, he thought, to Styles's wife to bed,
Nor knew his own was laid there in her stead:
Civilian, is the child he then begot
To be allow'd legitimate, or not?

MOTTO FOR A SUNDIAL   39

Give God thy heart,
Thy hopes,
Thy service and thy gold.
The day wears on
And Time is waxing old.

★ Lawyers practising Civil Law.

40   What is our life? a play of passion.
     Our mirth? the music of division.
     Our mothers' wombs the tiring houses be
     Where we are drest for life's short comedy.
     The earth the stage, heaven the spectator is,
     Who still doth note whoe'er do act amiss.
     Our graves that hide us from the all-seeing sun,
     Are but drawn curtains when the play is done.

41   ON TOM-O-COMBE

            Thin in beard, and thick in purse,
            Never man beloved worse,
            He went to the grave with many a curse.
            The devil and he had both one nurse.

42   ON THE DEATH OF THE LORD TREASURER

            Immoderate Death that wouldst not once confer,
            Nor talk, nor parley with the Treasurer:
            Had he been thee, or of thy faithful tribe,
            He would have spared thee, and tak'n a bribe.

HENRY PARROT
fl. 1600–1626

43   FATALES POETAE*

            Witches and poets co-embrace like fate,
            Reputed base, bare, poor, unfortunate.
            In these respects I may myself intrude
            Among the poets' thickest multitude.
                    * Fated Poets.

Here lies that poet, buried in the night,
Whose purse, men know it, was exceeding light.

THOMAS BASTARD
1566–1618

AD HENRICUM WOTTONEM* 45

Wotton, my little Bere dwells on a hill,
Under whose foot the silver trout doth swim,
The trout silver without and gold within,
Bibbing clear nectar, which doth aye distil
From Nulam's low head; there the birds are singing
And there the partial sun still gives occasion
To the sweet dew's eternal generation:
There is green joy and pleasure ever springing.
  O iron age of men, O time of rue,
    Shame ye not that all things are gold but you.

EPITAPH: *IOHANNIS SANDE*† 46

  Who would live in others' breath?
  Fame deceives the dead man's trust.
  Since our names are chang'd in death,
  Sand I was, and now am dust.

* To Henry Wotton.　　† Epitaph of John Sand.

Faustina hath a spot upon her face,
Mixed with sweet beauty making for her grace.
By what sweet influence it was begot,
I know not, but it is a spotless spot.

48   *IN GAETAM*

Gaeta from wool and weaving first began,
Swelling and swelling to a gentleman.
When he was gentleman, and bravely dight
He left not swelling till he was a knight.
At last (forgetting what he was at first)
    He swole to be a Lord: and then he burst.

JOHN HOSKYNS
1566–1638

49   ON A WHORE

One stone sufficeth (lo what death can do)
Her that in life was not content with two.

★ Of a mole on Faustina's face.

Here lies the man who in life
With every man had law and strife;
But now he is dead and laid in grave,
His bones no quiet rest can have,
For lay your ear unto this stone,
And you shall hear how every bone
Doth knock and beat against each other.
Pray for his soul's health, gentle brother.

OF THE LOSS OF TIME   51

If life be time that here is spent
And time on earth be cast away
Who so his time hath here misspent
Hath hasten'd his own dying day.
So it doth prove a killing crime
To massacre our living time.

If doing naught be like to death,
Of him that doth chameleon-wise
Take only pains to draw his breath,
The passers by may pasquilize,
      Not here he lives: but here he dies.

UPON ONE OF THE MAIDS OF   52
HONOUR TO QUEEN ELIZABETH

Here lies, the Lord have mercy upon her,
One of her Majesty's maids of honour:
She was both young, slender and pretty,
She died a maid, the more the pity.

Here lieth John Cruker, a maker of bellows,
His craft's master, and king of good fellows;
Yet when he came to the hour of his death,
He that made bellows, could not make breath.

54   HIS OWN EPITAPH, WHEN HE WAS SICK,
BEING FELLOW IN NEW COLLEGE, IN OXFORD

Reader, I would not have thee mistake:
Dead or alive I deserve not knowledge
Only but this, that my bones may make
Part of the dust of so worthy a college.

55   UPON A FOOL

Here lieth Thom Nick's body,
Who lived a fool and died a noddy:
As for his soul ask them that can tell,
Whether fools' souls go to heaven or to hell.

56   〈TO HIS SON BENNET, WRITTEN WHEN HE
WAS IN THE TOWER FOR JESTING AT THE
KING'S EXPENSE〉

My little Ben, whilst thou art young,
And know'st not how to rule thy tongue,
Make it thy slave whilst thou art free,
Lest it as mine imprison thee.

Here lyeth he, who was born and cried,
Told threescore years, fell sick, and died.

(after the Greek of Simonides)

Here lies the man that madly slain, 58
In earnest madness did complain,
On nature that she did not give
One life to lose, another to live.

⟨EPITAPH ON THE FART
IN THE PARLIAMENT HOUSE⟩ 59

Reader, I was born and cried,
Crackt so, smelt so, and so died,
Like to Caesar's was my death,
He in senate lost his breath;
And alike interr'd doth lie,
Thy famous Romulus and I.
And, at last, like Flora fair,
I left the commonwealth mine air.

* For a later version see No. 335.

EPITAPH
ON SIR WALTER PYE, ATTORNEY OF THE WARDS, DYING ON CHRISTMAS DAY, IN THE MORNING

If they ask, who here doth lie,
Say, 'tis the Devil's Christmas pie.
Death was the cook, the oven, the urn,
No ward for this, the Pye doth burn:
Yet serve it in, divers did wish
The Devil, long since, had had this dish.

SIR HENRY WOTTON
1568–1639

61   UPON THE DEATH OF SIR ALBERT MORTON'S WIFE

He first deceased; she for a little tried
To live without him, liked it not, and died.

SIR JOHN DAVIES
1569–1626

62   ON THE DEPUTY OF IRELAND'S CHILD

As careful mothers do to sleeping lay
Their babes which would too long the wantons play,
So to prevent my youth's approaching crimes,
Nature, my nurse, had me to bed betimes.

Liber doth vaunt how chastely he hath liv'd,
Since he hath bin seven years in town and more,
For that he swears he hath four only swiv'd,
A maid, a wife, a widow and a whore.
  Then, Liber, thou hast swiv'd all women kind,
  For a fift sort I know thou canst not find.

IN FUSCUM 64

Fuscus is free, and hath the world at will,
Yet in the course of life that he doth lead,
He's like a horse which turning round a mill,
Doth always in the selfsame circle tread:
First he doth rise at ten and at eleven
He goes to Giles, where he doth eat till one,
Then sees a play till six, and sups at seven,
And after supper, straight to bed is gone.
And there till ten next day he doth remain,
And then he dines, then sees a comedy,
And then he sups, and goes to bed again:
Thus round he runs without variety:
    Save that sometimes he comes not to the play
    But falls into a whore-house by the way.

Kate being pleas'd, wisht that her pleasure could
Indure as long as a buff jerkin would.
Content thee, Kate, although thy pleasure wasteth
Thy pleasure's place like a buff jerkin lasteth.
　　For no buff jerkin hath bin oftner worn
　　Nor hath more scrapings, or more dressings born.

66   *IN FRANCUM*

When Francus comes to solace with his whore,
He sends for rods and strips himself stark naked:
For his lust sleeps, and will not rise before,
By whipping of the wench, it be awaked.
　　　I envy him not, but wish I had the power
　　　To make myself his wench but one half hour.

ANONYMOUS
67   MY THREE WIVES

　　　Though marriage by some folks
　　　　　Be reckon'd a curse,
　　　Three wives I did marry
　　　　　For better or worse—
　　　The first for her person,
　　　　　The next for her purse,
　　　The third for a warming-pan,
　　　　　Doctress, and nurse.

　　　　　　　(*After the Latin of Étienne Pasquier*)

Here lies the good old knight Sir Harry,
Who loved well, but would not marry;
While he lived, and had his feeling,
She did lie, and he was kneeling,
Now he's dead and cannot feel
He doth lie and she doth kneel.

A CURE FOR POETRY   69

Seven wealthy towns contend for Homer dead,
Thro' which the living Homer begg'd his bread.

(After the Latin of George Buchanan)

Lais now old, that erst attempting lass,   70
To goddess Venus consecrates her glass;
For she herself hath now no use of one,
No dimpled cheeks hath she to gaze upon.
She cannot see her springtime damask grace,
Nor dare she look upon her winter face.

(After the Greek of Plato)★

★ For versions by Matthew Prior and Edwin Arlington Robinson see
Nos. 221 and 570.

The steed bit his master;
How came this to pass?
He heard the good pastor
Cry, All flesh is grass.

72   ON JOCKY BELL

I Jocky Bell o' Braikenbrow lyes under this stane,
Five of my awn sons laid it on my wame;
I liv'd aw my dayes but sturt or strife,
Was man o' my meat, and master o' my wife.
If you done better in your time than I did in mine,
Take this stane aff my wame, and lay it on o' thine.

73   Hic jacet Tom Shorthose,
          Sine tomb, sine sheets, sine riches,
          Qui vixit sine gown,
          Sine cloak, sine shirt, sine breeches.

74   TOBACCO

Tobacco is a filthy weed,
That from the devil doth proceed;
That drains your purse, that burns your clothes,
That makes a chimney of your nose.

Of woods, of plains, of hills and dales,
Of fields, of meads, of parks and pales,
Of all I had, this I possess,
I need no more, I have no less.

BEN JONSON
1573?–1637

TO DOCTOR EMPIRIC 76

When men a dangerous disease did 'scape
Of old, they gave a cock to Aesculape.
Let me give two, that doubly am got free
From my disease's danger, and from thee.

ON DON SURLY 77

Don Surly, to aspire the glorious name
Of a great man, and to be thought the same,
Makes serious use of all great trade he knows.
He speaks to men with a rhinocerote's nose,
Which he thinks great; and so reads verses, too;
And that is done, as he saw great men do.
H'has tympanies of business in his face,
And can forget men's names, with a great grace.
He will both argue and discourse in oaths,
Both which are great. And laugh at ill made clothes—
That's greater yet—to cry his own up neat.
He doth, at meals, alone, his pheasant eat,
Which is main greatness. And, at his still-board,
He drinks to no man; that's, too, like a lord.

He keeps another's wife, which is a spice
Of solemn greatness. And he dares, at dice,
Blaspheme God, greatly. Or some poor hind beat,
That breathes in his dog's way: and this is great.
Nay more, for greatness' sake, he will be one
May hear my *Epigrams*, but like of none.
Surly, use other arts, these only can
Style thee a great fool, but no great man.

78   TO FOOL, OR KNAVE

Thy praise, or dispraise is to me alike,
One doth not stroke me, nor the other strike.

79   TO FINE LADY WOULD-BE

Fine Madam Would-be, wherefore should you fear
That love to make so well, a child to bear?
The world reputes you barren: but I know
Your 'pothecary, and his drugs say no.
Is it the pain affrights? that's soon forgot.
Or your complexion's loss? you have a pot
That can restore that. Will it hurt your feature?
To make amends, you're thought a wholesome creature.
What should the cause be? Oh, you live at court:
And there's both loss of time, and loss of sport
In a great belly. Write, then, on thy womb:
Of the not born, yet buried, here's the tomb.

Here lies to each her parents' ruth,
Mary, the daughter of their youth;
Yet all heaven's gifts being heaven's due,
It makes the father less to rue.
At six months' end, she parted hence
With safety of her innocence;
Whose soul heaven's Queen (whose name she bears)
In comfort of her mother's tears,
Hath plac'd amongst her virgin-train:
Where, while that sever'd doth remain,
This grave partakes the fleshly birth.
Which cover lightly, gentle earth.

ON MY FIRST SON 81

Farewell, thou child of my right hand, and joy;
My sin was too much hope of thee, lov'd boy,
Seven years thou wert lent to me, and I thee pay,
Exacted by thy fate, on the just day.
O, could I lose all father, now. For why
Will man lament the state he should envie?
To have so soon scap'd World's and flesh's rage,
And, if no other misery, yet age?
Rest in soft peace, and, ask'd, say here doth lie
Ben Jonson his best piece of poetrie.
For whose sake, henceforth, all his vows be such,
As what he loves may never live too much.

Reader, stay,
And if I had no more to say
But here doth lie till the last day
All that is left of Philip Gray,
It might thy patience richly pay:
For, if such men as he could die,
What surety of life have thou, and I?

83   MARTIAL. EPIGRAM XLVII, BOOK X*

The things that make the happier life, are these,
Most pleasant Martial: Substance got with ease,
Not labour'd for, but left thee by thy sire;
A soil not barren; a continual fire;
Never at law; seldom in office gown'd;
A quiet mind; free powers; and body sound;
A wise simplicity; friends alike-stated;
Thy table without art, and easy-rated;
Thy night not drunken, but from cares laid waste;
No sour, or sullen bed-mate, yet a chaste;
Sleep, that will make the darkest hours swift-pac'd;
Will to be, what thou art; and nothing more;
Nor fear thy latest day, nor wish therefor.

* See No. 8, for a version by Henry Howard, Earl of Surrey.

Would'st thou hear what man can say
In a little? Reader, stay.
Underneath this stone doth lie
As much beauty, as could die:
Which in life did harbour give
To more virtue, than doth live.
If at all she had a fault,
Leave it buried in this vault.
One name was Elizabeth,
The other let it sleep with death:
Fitter, where it died, to tell
Than that it liv'd at all. Farewell.

SIR JOHN YOUNG
fl. 1635

⟨ON BEN JONSON, IN WESTMINSTER ABBEY⟩   85

O rare Ben Jonson!

JOHN DONNE
1573–1631

A SELF ACCUSER   86

Your mistress, that you follow whores, still taxeth you:
'Tis strange that she should thus confess it, though 't be true.

PHRYNE   87

Thy flattering picture, Phryne, is like thee,
Only in this, that you both painted be.

JOHN WEEVER
1576–1632
88   *DE SE**

> Some men marriage do commend,
> And all their life in wiving spend;
> But if that I should wives have three
> (God keep me from polygamie)
>   I'll give the devil two for pay,
>   If he will fetch the third away.

SIR THOMAS ROE
1581?–1644
89   ON GUSTAVUS ADOLPHUS,
                    KING OF SWEDEN

> Upon this place the great Gustavus died,
> While Victory lay weeping by his side.

RICHARD CORBET
1582–1635
90   LITTLE LUTE

> (Upon one coming to visit his mistress, and she
>   being absent, he wrote:)

> Little lute, when I am gone,
> Tell thy mistress here was one
> That did come with full intent
> To play upon her instrument.

> (The said mistress, going to visit him at his chamber
> in his absence, she wrote on one of his books thus:)
>   * Of himself.

Little book, when I am gone,
Tell thy master here was one
That in her heart would be content
To be at his commandement.

FRANCIS BEAUMONT
1584–1616

UPON MASTER EDMUND SPENSER, THE   91
FAMOUS POET

At Delphos shrine one did a doubt propound,
Which by the oracle must be released,
Whether of poets were the best renown'd,
Those that survive, or those that be deceased.
The god made answer by divine suggestion,
While Spenser is alive, it is no question.

WILLIAM DRUMMOND OF HAWTHORNDEN
1585–1649

EPITAPH   92
⟨On Lord Sanquhar, hanged at Westminster, for murder, in 1612⟩

Sanquhar, whom this earth could scarce contain,
Having seen Italy, France, and Spain,
To finish his travels, a spectacle rare,
Was bound towards heaven, but died in the air.

93   TO A COVETOUS CHURL

Although thy blood be frozen, and thy scalp
Exceed the whiteness of the snowy Alp,
Though thy few teeth can hardly chew the crumb,
Though to the Stygian lake thou now art come,
And though one leg is now within the grave,
Yet still more gold thou dost desire to have:
What dost thou mean? Know Charon does not care
For all thy wealth, one penny is his fare.

94   FIVE THINGS WHITE

Four things are white, the fifth exceeds the rest,
Snow, silver, ceruse, age, and a chaste breast.

95   TO BARBA

Have I the power to bid the frost not melt,
Or Alpine snow, when it the sun hath felt?
Or can I stay the falling showers of rain,
When springy exhalations drop again?
Or may I mask the stars, or Cynthia bright,
In a fair evening, and a frosty night?
No more have I the power to enforce
Thy constancy, for lust will have its course.

Behold, my dearest, how the fragrant rose
Is fresh and blown, whilst on the tree it grows;
But being by some rude hand pluck'd away,
Loseth its sweetness, and doth soon decay:
Even so poor I, or live, or die by thee,
I am thy rose, my dear, and thou my tree.

TO CERTAIN MAIDENS PLAYING WITH SNOW 97

You tender virgins, fairer than the snow with which you play,
Note how it melts, think how the roses grow, and how decay,
Just so does beauty fade, and age draw on,
Winter makes haste, and summer's quickly gone.

(From the Latin of John Parkhurst)

ROBERT HERRICK
1591–1674
AN EPITAPH UPON A VIRGIN 98

Here a solemn fast we keep,
While all beauty lies asleep
Hush'd be all things; no noise here
But the toning of a tear:
Or a sigh of such as bring
Cowslips for her covering.

Love is a circle that doth restless move
In the same sweet eternity of love.

100 ## ON HIMSELF

Born I was to meet with age,
And to walk life's pilgrimage,
Much, I know, of time is spent,
Tell I can't what's resident.
Howsoever, cares, adieu;
I'll have nought to say to you:
But I'll spend my coming hours
Drinking wine, and crown'd with flowers.

101 ## A FROLIC

Bring me my rose-buds, drawer, come;
    So while I thus sit crown'd,
I'll drink the aged Cecubum,
    Until the roof turn round.

Here she lies (in bed of spice)
Fair as Eve in Paradise:
For her beauty it was such
Poets could not praise too much.
Virgins come, and in a ring
Her supremest requiem sing;
Then depart, but see ye tread
Lightly, lightly o'er the dead.

AN EPITAPH UPON A CHILD 103

Virgins promis'd when I died,
That they would each primrose-tide,
Duly, morn and ev'ning, come,
And with flowers dress my tomb.
Having promis'd, pay your debts,
Maids, and here strew violets.

THE COMING OF GOOD LUCK 104

So Good Luck came, and on my roof did light,
Like noiseless snow; or as the dew of night:
Not all at once, but gently, as the trees
Are, by the sunbeams, tickled by degrees.

LONG AND LAZY 105

That was the proverb. Let my mistress be
Lazy to others, but be long to me.

'Tis still observ'd, that Fame ne'er sings
The order, but the sum of things.

107   MODERATION

In things a moderation keep,
Kings ought to shear, not skin their sheep.

108   UPON SCOBBLE. EPIGRAM

Scobble for whoredom whips his wife; and cries,
He'll slit her nose; but blubb'ring she replies,
Good Sir, make no more cuts i' th' outward skin,
One slit's enough to let adultry in.

109   UPON BATT

Batt he gets children, not for love to rear 'em;
But out of hope his wife might die to bear 'em.

110   UPON BEN JONSON

Here lies Jonson with the rest
Of the poets; but the best.
Reader, wouldst thou more have known?
Ask his story, not this stone.
That will speak what this can't tell
Of his glory. *So farewell.*

Here I myself might likewise die,
And utterly forgotten lie,
But that eternal Poetrie
Repullulation gives me here
Unto the thirtieth thousand year,
When all now dead shall re-appear.

ON HIMSELF   112

Weep for the dead, for they have lost this light;
And weep for me, lost in an endless night.
Or mourn, or make a marble verse for me,
Who writ for many. *Benedicite.*

FRANCIS QUARLES
1592–1644

OF COMMON DEVOTION   113

Our God and soldiers we alike adore,
Ev'n at the brink of danger; not before:
After deliverance, both alike requited,
Our God's forgotten, and our soldiers slighted.

My soul, what's lighter than a feather? Wind.   114
Than wind? The fire. And what than fire? The mind.
What's lighter than the mind? A thought. Than thought?
This bubble world. What than this bubble? Nought.

115   ON JUDAS ISCARIOT

> Some curse that traitor Judas life and limb:
> God knows, some curse themselves, in cursing him.

116   ON OFF'RINGS

> Are all such off'rings, as are crusht, and bruis'd,
> Forbid thy altar? May they not be us'd?
> And must all broken things be set apart?
> No, Lord: Thou wilt accept a broken heart.

HUGH HOLLAND
d. 1633

117   EPITAPH ON PRINCE HENRY

> Lo now he shineth yonder,
> A fixed star in heaven,
> Whose motion is under
> None of the planets seven;
>   And if the sun should tender
>   The moon his love and marry,
>   They never could engender
>   So fair a star as Harry.

ANONYMOUS

118   ON BUTTON THE GRAVE-MAKER

> Ye powers above and heavenly poles,
> Are graves become but Button-holes?

We lived one and twenty year
   As man and wife together:
I could not stay her longer here,
   She's gone I know not whither;
But this I know, I do protest,
   (I speak it not to flatter)
Of all the women in the world,
   I swear I'd ne'er come at her.
Her body is bestowed well,
   This handsome grave doth hide her,
And sure her soul is not in hell,
   The devil could ne'er abide her:
But I suppose she's soar'd aloft,
   For in the late great thunder,
Methought I heard her very voice,
   Rending the clouds asunder.

UPON A PURITANICAL LOCKSMITH   120

A zealous locksmith died of late,
And did arrive at heaven gate,
He stood without and would not knock,
Because he meant to pick the lock.

121 ON THOMAS TURNER, MASTER OF THE COMPANY OF BAKERS, BRISTOL

Like to a baker's oven is the grave,
Wherein the bodies of the faithful have
A setting in, and where they do remain,
In hopes to rise, and to be drawn again.
Blessed are they who in the Lord are dead,
Though set like dough, they shall be drawn like bread.

WILLIAM BROWNE OF TAVISTOCK
1592–1643?

122 EPITAPH
IN OBITUM M.S., X MAII, 1614★

May! Be thou never grac'd with birds that sing,
Nor Flora's pride!
In thee all flowers and roses spring.
Mine only died.

123 EPITAPH ON THE COUNTESS DOWAGER OF PEMBROKE

Underneath this sable hearse
Lies the subject of all verse:
Sidney's sister, Pembroke's mother:
Death, ere thou hast slain another
Fair, and learn'd, and good as she,
Time shall throw a dart at thee.

★ On the death of M.S., 10 May, 1614.

ON MR. PRICKE 124

Upon the fifth day of November
Christ's College lost a privy member;
Cupid and death did both their arrows nick,
Cupid shot short, but death did hit the prick;
Women lament, and maidens make great moans,
Because the prick is laid beneath the stones.

ON MEETING A GENTLEWOMAN 125
IN THE DARK

To see such dainty ghosts as you appear
Will make my flesh stand sooner than my hair.

INVITATION TO DALLIANCE 126

Be not thou so foolish nice,
As to be intreated twice;
What should women more incite
Than their own sweet appetite?

Shall savage things more freedom have
Than nature unto women gave?
The swan, the turtle, and the sparrow
Bill awhile, then take the marrow.
    They bill, they kiss, what else they do
    Come bill, and kiss, and I'll show you.

A light young man lay with a lighter woman,
And did request their things might be in common;
And gave her (when her good will he had gotten)
A yard of Holland for an ell of Cotton.

BARTEN HOLYDAY
1593–1661

128   ⟨IRELAND⟩

Bogs, purgatory, wolves and ease, by fame
Are counted Ireland's earth, mistake, curse, shame.

129   ⟨PRIDE⟩

Pride cannot see itself by mid-day light:
The peacock's tail is furthest from his sight!

130   ⟨MANKIND⟩

Clay, sand, and rock, seem of a diff'rent birth:
So men; some stiff, some loose, some firm: All earth!

⟨THE VOICE OF ARDENT ZEAL SPEAKS   131
FROM THE LOLLARD'S TOWER OF
ST. PAUL'S⟩

To see a strange outlandish fowl,
A quaint baboon, an ape, an owl,
A dancing bear, a giant's bone,
A foolish engine move alone,
A morris-dance, a puppet-play,
Mad Tom to sing a roundelay,
A woman dancing on a rope,
Bull-baiting also at the *Hope*,
A rhymer's jests, a juggler's cheats,
A tumbler showing cunning feats,
Or players acting on the stage—
There goes the bounty of our age:
   But unto any pious notion,
   There's little coin and less devotion.

EPITAPH ON THE LADY MARY VILLIERS   132

The Lady Mary Villiers lies
Under this stone; with weeping eyes
The parents that first gave her birth,
And their sad friends, laid her in earth.
If any of them, Reader, were
Known unto thee, shed a tear;
Or if thyself possess a gem
As dear to thee, as this to them,

Though a stranger to this place,
Bewail in theirs thine own hard case:
For thou, perhaps, at thy return
Mayest find thy darling in an urn.

JAMES SHIRLEY
1596–1666

133   ON THE DUKE OF BUCKINGHAM

Here lies the best and worst of fate,
Two kings' delight, the people's hate,
The courtiers' star, the kingdom's eye,
A man to draw an angel by,
 Fear's despiser, Villiers' glory,
  The great man's volume, all time's story.

WILLIAM STRODE
1602–1645

134   My love and I for kisses play'd,
She would keep stake, I was content,
But when I won she would be paid;
This made me ask her what she meant.
Pray, since I see (quoth she) your wrangling vein,
Take your own kisses, give me mine again.

THOMAS RANDOLPH
1605–1635

135   This definition poetry doth fit,
It is a witty madness, or mad wit.

ONE IN THE GOUT WISHING FOR KING   136
PYRRHUS HIS TOE, WHICH COULD NOT
BE BURNT AT HIS FUNERAL PYRE

O for a toe, such as the funeral pyre
Could make no work on, proof against flame and fire
Which lay unburnt when all the rest burnt out,
Such amianthine toes might scorn the gout;
And the most powerful blast the gout could blow
Prove but an *ignis lambens* to that toe.

In yellow meadows I take no delight: 137
Let me have those which are most red and white.

EDMUND WALLER
1606–1687

TO ONE MARRIED TO AN OLD MAN   138

Since thou wouldst needs (bewitch'd with some ill charms!)
Be buried in those monumental arms,
All we can wish is, may that earth lie light
Upon thy tender limbs! and so good night.

SIR ASTON COKAYNE
1608–1684

139   EPITAPH ON A GREAT SLEEPER

Here lies a great sleeper, as everybody knows,
Whose soul would not care if his body ne'er rose,
The business of life he hated, and chose
To die for his ease for his better repose;
And 'tis believed, when the last trump doth wake him,
Had the Devil a bed, he would pray him to take him.

JOHN MILTON
1608–1674

140   AN EPITAPH ON THE ADMIRABLE
             DRAMATIC POET, W. SHAKESPEARE

What needs my Shakespeare for his honour'd bones,
The labour of an age in piled stones,
Or that his hallow'd relics should be hid
Under a star-ypointing pyramid?
Dear son of memory, great heir of fame,
What need'st thou such weak witness of thy name?
Thou in our wonder and astonishment
Hast built thy self a live-long monument.
For whilst to th' shame of slow-endeavouring art,
Thy easy numbers flow, and that each heart
Hath from the leaves of thy unvalu'd book,
Those Delphic lines with deep impression took,
Then thou our fancy of itself bereaving,
Dost make us marble with too much conceiving;
And so sepulcher'd in such pomp dost lie,
That kings for such a tomb would wish to die.

who sicken'd in the time of his vacancy, being forbid to go to
London, by reason of the Plague

Here lies old Hobson, Death hath broke his girt,
And here alas, hath laid him in the dirt,
Or else the ways being foul, twenty to one,
He's here stuck in a slough, and overthrown.
'Twas such a shifter, that if truth were known,
Death was half glad when he had got him down;
For he had any time this ten years full,
Dodg'd with him, betwixt Cambridge and the Bull.
And surely, Death could never have prevail'd,
Had not his weekly course of carriage fail'd;
But lately finding him so long at home,
And thinking now his journey's end was come,
And that he had tane up his latest inn,
In the kind office of a chamberlin
Shew'd him his room where he must lodge that night,
Pull'd off his boots, and took away the light:
If any ask for him, it shall be said,
Hobson has supped, and's newly gone to bed.

SIR JOHN SUCKLING
1609–1642

THE METAMORPHOSIS   142

The little Boy, to shew his might and power,
Turn'd Io to a cow, Narcissus to a flower;
Transform'd Apollo to a homely swain,
And Jove himself into a golden rain.
    These shapes were tolerable, but by th' mass
    He's metamorphos'd me into an ass!

ROBERT WILD
1609–1679

143   EPITAPH FOR A GODLY MAN'S TOMB

> Here lies a piece of Christ; a star in dust;
> A vein of gold; a china dish that must
> Be used in heaven, when God shall feast the just.

ANONYMOUS

144   Oh, England. Sick in head and sick in heart,
> Sick in whole and every part,
> And yet sicker thou art still
> For thinking, that thou art not ill.

ROWLAND WATKYNS
c. 1610–1664

145   ⟨BAD COMPANY⟩

> Bad company is a disease;
> Who lies with dogs, shall rise with fleas.

146   UPON SAUL SEEKING HIS FATHER'S ASSES

> Saul did much care and diligence express,
> By seeking asses in the wilderness;
> Three days he travell'd with a serious mind
> To find them out, but could no asses find:
> Find out a hundred you in London may
> Of Presbyterian asses in one day.

I love him not; but shew no reason can
Wherefore, but this, *I do not love the man.*

(*After the Latin of Martial*)

STRANGE MONSTERS 148

Of diverse monsters I have sometimes read,
Some without feet, and some without a head.
No fouler monsters can hot Africk bring,
Than rebels are without their head the King.

WORLDLY WEALTH 149
Natura paucis contenta†

Wealth unto every man, I see,
Is like the bark unto the tree:
Take from the tree the bark away,
The naked tree will soon decay.
Lord, make me not too rich, nor make me poor,
To wait at rich mens' tables, or their door.

★ See also the more famous version by Tom Brown, No. 199.
† Nature is content with little.

JAMES GRAHAM, MARQUIS OF MONTROSE
1612–1650

150   VERSES COMPOSED ON THE EVE OF
HIS EXECUTION

Let them bestow on every airth a limb,
Then open all my veins that I may swim
To thee, my Maker, in that crimson lake;
Then place my parboiled head upon a stake,
Scatter my ashes, strew them in the air—
Lord! since thou knowest where all these atoms are,
I'm hopeful thou'lt recover once my dust,
And confident thou'lt raise me with the just.

SAMUEL BUTLER
1612–1680

151   An ass will with his long ears fray
The flies, that tickle him, away;
But Man delights to have his ears
Blown maggots in by flatterers.

152   The greatest saints and sinners have been made
Of proselytes of one another's trade.

153   A great philosopher did choke
With laughing at a jest he broke.

154   Far greater numbers have been lost by hopes,
Than all the magazines of daggers, ropes,
And other ammunitions of despair,
Were ever able to dispatch, by fear.

A convert's but a fly, that turns about,   155
After his head's pull'd off, to find it out.

Authority is a disease, and cure,   156
Which men can neither want, nor well endure.

What makes all subjects discontent   157
Against a prince's government?
And princes take as great offence
At subjects' disobedience?
That neither the other can abide,
But too much reason on each side?

A married man comes nearest to the dead,   158
And to be buried's but to go to bed.

The Devil was more generous than Adam,   159
That never laid the fault upon his madam:
But like a gallant and heroic elf
Took freely all the crime upon himself.

Here lies the corpse of William Prynne,
A bencher late of Lincoln's Inn,
Who restless ran through thick and thin.

This grand scripturient paper-spiller,
This endless, needless margin-filler,
Was strangely tost from post to pillar.

His brain's career was never stopping,
But pen with rheum of gall still dropping,
Till hand o'er head brought ears to cropping.

Nor would he yet surcease such themes,
But prostitute new virgin reams
To types of his fanatic dreams.

But whilst he this hot humour hugs,
And for more length of tedder tugs,
Death fang'd the remnant of his lugs.

161   Hypocrisy will serve as well
To propagate a church, as zeal;
As persecution and promotion
Do equally advance devotion:
So round white stones will serve, they say,
As well as eggs to make hens lay.

RICHARD CRASHAW
1613–1649
162   ON MARRIAGE

I would be married, but I'd have no wife,
I would be married to a single life.

To these, whom Death again did wed,
This grave's their second marriage-bed,
For though the hand of Fate could force
'Twixt soul and body a divorce,
It could not sunder man and wife,
'Cause they both liv'd but one life.
Peace, good reader, do not weep.
Peace, the lovers are asleep.
They, sweet turtles, folded lie
In the last knot love could tie.
And though they lie as they were dead,
Their pillow stone, their sheets of lead
(Pillow hard, and sheets not warm),
Love made the bed; they'll take no harm.
Let them sleep, let them sleep on,
Till this stormy night be gone,
And th' eternal morrow dawn;
Then the curtains will be drawn
And they wake into a light,
Whose day shall never die in night.

ON THE BAPTIZED AETHIOPIAN   164

Let it no longer be a forlorn hope
     To wash an Aethiope:
He's washt, his gloomy skin a peaceful shade
     For his white soul is made:
And now, I doubt not, the Eternal Dove
     A black-fac'd house will have.

Here where our Lord once laid his head,
Now the grave lies buried.

JOHN CLEVELAND
1613–1658

166   EPITAPH ON THE EARL OF STRAFFORD

Here lies wise and valiant dust,
Huddled up 'twixt fit and just:
Strafford, who was hurried hence
'Twixt treason and convenience.
He spent his time here in a mist,
A Papist, yet a Calvinist;
His Prince's nearest joy and grief:
He had, yet wanted, all relief:
The prop and ruin of the state,
The people's violent love and hate.
One in extremes lov'd and abhorr'd.
Riddles lie here, or in a word,
Here lies blood, and let it lie
Speechless still, and never cry.

SIR JOHN DENHAM
1615–1669

167   Had Cowley ne'er spoke, Killigrew ne'er writ,
Combin'd in one, they'd made a matchless wit.

To-morrow you will live, you always cry;   168
In what far country does this morrow lie,
That 'tis so mighty long ere it arrive?
Beyond the Indies does this morrow live?

'Tis so far fetch'd this morrow, that I fear
'Twill be both very old and very dear.
To-morrow I will live, the fool does say;
To-day itself's too late, the wise liv'd yesterday.

(After the Latin of Martial)

EPITAPH OF PYRAMUS AND THISBE   169

I

Underneath this marble stone
Lie two beauties join'd in one,

II

Two whose loves Death could not sever,
For both liv'd, both died together.

III

Two white souls, being too divine
For earth, in their own sphere now shine,

IV

Who have left their loves to fame,
And their earth to earth again.

RICHARD LOVELACE
1618–1658

170   A fool much bit by fleas put out the light,
         You shall not see me now (quoth he), good night.

                                        (*From the Greek of Lucian*)

THOMAS STANLEY
1625–1678

171   ON A SEAL

         Five oxen, grazing in a flow'ry mead,
         A jasper seal (done to the life) doth hold;
         The little herd away long since had fled,
         Were't not enclos'd within a pale of gold.

                                        (*After the Greek of Plato*)

172   LOVE SLEEPING

         Within the covert of a shady grove,
         We saw the little red-cheek'd God of Love.
         He had nor bow nor quiver, those among
         The neighb'ring trees upon a bough were hung:
         Upon a bank of tender rose-buds laid
         He, smiling slept; bees with their noise invade
         His rest, and on his lips their honey made.

                                        (*After the Greek of Plato*)

Would I were air that thou with heat opprest   173
Might'st let me breathe myself into thy breast.

(From the Greek Anthology)

PAN PIPING   174

Dwell, awful Silence, on the shady hills
Among the bleating flocks, and purling rills,
When Pan the reed doth to his lips apply,
Inspiring it with sacred harmony.
Hydriads, and Hamadryads at that sound
In a well order'd measure beat the ground.

(After the Greek of Plato)

THE LEAVES COME AGAIN   175

In March birds couple, a new birth
Of herbs and flowers breaks through the earth,
But in the grave none stirs his head;
Long is th'impris'ment of the dead.

(from the Welsh)

CHARLES COTTON
1630–1687

MADRIGAL

To be a whore, despite of grace,
Good counsel and an ugly face,
And to distribute still the pox,
    To men of wit
Will seem a kind of paradox;
    And yet
Thou art a whore, despite of grace,
Good counsel and an ugly face.

177 AN EPITAPH ON M.H.

In this cold monument lies one,
That I know who has laid upon,
The happier he: her sight would charm,
And touch have kept King David warm.
Lovely, as is the dawning East,
Was this marble's frozen guest;
As soft, and snowy, as that down
Adorns the blow-ball's frizzled crown;
As straight and slender as the crest,
Or antlet of the one-beam'd beast;
Pleasant as th'odorous month of May:
As glorious, and as light as day.

    Whom I admir'd, as soon as knew,
And now her memory pursue
With such a superstitious lust,
That I could fumble with her dust.

She all perfections had, and more,
Tempting, as if design'd a whore,
For so she was; and since there are
Such, I could wish them all as fair.

Pretty she was, and young, and wise,
And in her calling so precise,
That industry had made her prove
The sucking school-mistress of love:
And Death, ambitious to become
Her pupil, left his ghastly home,
And, seeing how we us'd her here,
The raw-boned rascal ravisht her.

Who, pretty soul, resign'd her breath,
To seek new lechery in Death.

JOHN DRYDEN
1631–1700

⟨ON JACOB TONSON, HIS PUBLISHER⟩   178

With leering looks, bullfac'd, and freckled fair,
With two left legs, and Judas-colour'd hair,
With frowzy pores, that taint the ambient air.

179   EPITAPH ON THE DUKE OF GRAFTON

Here
Lies a peer
Beneath this place
Styl'd His Grace
The Duke of Grafton,
A blade as fine, as e'er had haft on.
Mark'd with a Garter and a Star,
Forg'd out, and ground for war;
Of mettle true
As ever drew,
Or made a pass
At lad or lass.
This valiant son of Mars
Ne'er hung an arse
With sword or tarse,
Nor turn'd his tail,
Tho' shots like hail
Flew about his ears
With spikes and spears
So thick, they'd hide the sun.
He boldly forc'd his way
Leading the van
More like the devil than a man:
For why, he valu'd not a fart a gun,
He ne'er would dread
Bullets of lead,
Nor cannon ball
Nothing at all;
But a bullet of cork
Soon did his work,

Unhappy pellet,
With grief I tell it,
For with one blow thou hast undone
Great Caesar's son:
A soldier foil'd,
A statesman spoil'd.
God rot him
That shot him
For a son of a whore,
I'll say no more,
But here lies Henry, Duke of Grafton.

CHARLES SACKVILLE, EARL OF DORSET
1638–1706

Cloe's the wonder of her sex: 180
   'Tis well her heart is tender;
How might such killing eyes perplex,
   With virtue to defend her?

But nature, graciously inclin'd,
   Not bent to vex, but please us,
Has, to her boundless beauty, join'd
   A boundless will to ease us.

PHILIP AYRES
1638–1712

FAIR AND SOFTLY   181

The yoke uneasy on the ox doth sit
   Till by degrees his stubborn neck does bow.
So Love's opposers do at last submit
   And gladly drudge at the accustom'd plough.

Since Man's a little world, to make it great
Add Woman, and the metaphor's complete;
Nature this piece with utmost skill design'd,
And made her of a substance more refin'd,
But wretched Man, compos'd of dust and clay,
Must like all earthly things, with time decay;

> While she may justly boast of what's eternal,
> A heav'nly count'nance, and a heart infernal.

SIR CHARLES SEDLEY
1639?–1701

183   TO SERGIUS

Thou'lt fight, if any man call Thebe whore:
That she is thine, what can proclaim it more.

184   ON A COCK AT ROCHESTER

Thou cursed cock, with thy perpetual noise,
May'st thou be capon made, and lose thy voice,
Or on a dunghill may'st thou spend thy blood,
And vermin prey upon thy craven brood;
May rivals tread thy hens before thy face,
Then with redoubled courage give thee chase;
May'st thou be punish'd for St. Peter's crime,
And on Shrove Tuesday, perish in thy prime;
May thy bruis'd carcass be some beggar's feast,
Thou first and worst disturber of man's rest.

Thou swear'st thou'lt drink no more; kind Heaven send
Me such a cook or coachman, but no friend.

(After the Latin of Martial)

TO SEXTUS 186

What business, or what hope brings thee to town,
    Who can'st not pimp, nor cheat, nor swear, nor lie?
This place will nourish no such idle drone;
    Hence, in remoter parts thy fortune try.
But thou hast courage, honesty, and wit,
    And one, or all these three, will give thee bread:
The malice of this town thou know'st not yet;
    Wit is a good diversion, but base trade;
Cowards will, for thy courage, call thee bully,
    Till all, like Thraso's, thy acquaintance shun;
Rogues call thee for thy honesty a cully;
    Yet this is all thou hast to live upon:
Friend, three such virtues Audley had undone;
    Be wise, and ere th'art in a jail, be gone.
Of all that starving crew we saw to-day
None but has kill'd his man, or writ his play.

(After the Latin of Martial)

Dear Friend, I fear my heart will break;
In t'other world I scarce believe,
In this I little pleasure take:
That my whole grief thou may'st conceive;
Could not I drink more than I whore,
By heaven, I would not live an hour.

188   TO SCILLA

Storm not, brave friend, that thou hadst never yet
        Mistress nor wife that others did not swive,
But, like a Christian, pardon and forget,
        For thy own pox will thy revenge contrive.

189   TO NYSUS

How shall we please this age? If in a song
We put above six lines, they count it long;
If we contract it to an epigram,
As deep the dwarfish poetry they damn;
If we write plays, few see above an act,
And those lewd masks, or noisy fops, distract:
Let us write satire then, and at our ease
Vex th'ill-natur'd fools we cannot please.

HENRY ALDRICH
1647–1710

If all be true that I do think,   190
There are five reasons we should drink:
Good wine—a friend—or being dry—
Or lest we should be by and by—
Or any other reason why.

(After the Latin of Jacques Sirmond)

ANONYMOUS

CHARLES II   191

Of a tall stature, and of sable hue,
Much like the son of Kish, that lofty Jew,
Twelve years complete he suffered in exile,
And kept his father's asses all the while.

ON THE MEETINGS OF THE   192
SCOTCH COVENANTERS

Informer, art thou in the tree,
Take heed lest there thou hangèd be;
Look likewise to thy foothold well
Lest, if thou slip, thou fall to hell.

JOHN WILMOT, EARL OF ROCHESTER
1647–1680

193   WRITTEN ON THE MANUSCRIPT OF
HEROD AND MARIAMNE SUBMITTED
FOR HIS LORDSHIP'S APPROVAL

> Poet, whoe'er thou art, God damn thee;
> Go hang thyself, and burn thy *Mariamne*.

194   ⟨ON KING CHARLES THE SECOND⟩

> God bless our good and gracious King,
>   Whose promise none relies on;
> Who never said a foolish thing,
>   Nor ever did a wise one.

ANONYMOUS

195   FADING BEAUTY

> Take time, my dear, ere Time takes wing;
> Beauty knows no second spring;
> Marble pillars, tombs of brass,
> Time breaks down, much more this glass;
> Then ere that tyrant Time bespeak it,
> Let's drink healths in't first, then break it.
>   At twenty-five in women's eyes
>   Beauty does fade, at thirty dies.

Once in our lives,
Let us drink to our wives,
Though the number of them is but small
God take the best,
And the devil take the rest,
And so we shall be rid of them all.

VERSES PINN'D TO A SHEET, IN WHICH A   197
LADY STOOD TO DO PENANCE IN THE CHURCH

Here stand I, for whores as great
  To cast a scornful eye on:
Should each whore here be doom'd a sheet,
  You'd soon want one to lie on.

NATHANIEL LEE
1653?–1692

NATHANIEL LEE TO SIR ROGER L'ESTRANGE,   198
WHO VISITED HIM IN HIS MADHOUSE

Faces may alter, names can't change:
I am strange Lee altered; you are still L'E-Strange.

TOM BROWN
1663–1704

DOCTOR FELL*   199

I do not love thee, Doctor Fell.
The reason why, I cannot tell;
But this I know, and know full well,
I do not love thee, Doctor Fell.

(After the Latin of Martial)

* For another version, see No. 147.

Reader, beneath this turf I lie,
    And behold myself content,
Piss, if you please, pray what care I,
    Since now my life is spent:

A marble stone indeed, might keep
    My body from the weather,
And gather people as I sleep,
    And call more fools together.

But hadst thou been from whence I came,
    Thou'dst never mince the matter,
But shew thy sentiments the same,
    And hate stone-doublets after.

I'm dead, and that's enough t' acquaint
    A man of any sense,
That if he's looking for a saint,
    He must go further hence.

Between two roses down I fell
    As 'twixt two stools a platter,
One held me up exceeding well,
    T'other did no such matter:

The Rose by Temple-Bar gave wine,
    Exchang'd for chalk, and fill'd me;
But being for the ready coin,
    The Rose in Wood Street kill'd me.

---

stone-doublet: prison. exchanged for chalk: on tick (chalked up). The
Rose in Wood Street: the Wood Street Compter, or debtors' prison.

The Colonels here in solemn manner meet,
Not with a full design the French to beat,
But to consult where they may nicely eat,
What trusting mortals sell the noblest wine,
Where, free from duns, they may securely dine.

Our fathers took oaths as of old they took wives,　　202
To have and to hold for the term of their lives,
But we take our oaths, as our whores, for our ease,
And a whore and a rogue may part when they please.

ANONYMOUS
⟨KING WILLIAM THE THIRD TO HIMSELF⟩　203

As I walk'd by my self
And talk'd to my self,
My self said unto me,
Look to thy self,
Take care of thy self,
For nobody cares for thee.

I answer'd my self,
And said to my self,
In the self-same repartee,
Look to thy self
Or not look to thy self,
The self-same thing will be.

Here lies Fuller's
Earth.

205   ⟨ON WILLIAM WALKER, AUTHOR OF
     "A TREATISE OF ENGLISH PARTICLES"⟩

Here lie Walker's particles.

MATTHEW PRIOR
1664–1721

206   PHYLLIS'S AGE

How old may Phyllis be, you ask,
    Whose beauty thus all hearts engages?
To answer is no easy task,
    For she has really two ages.

Stiff in brocard, and pinch'd in stays,
    His patches, paint, and jewels on,
All day let envy view her face;
    And Phyllis is but twenty-one.

Paint, patches, jewels laid aside,
    As night astronomers agree,
The evening has the day belied;
    And Phyllis is some forty-three.

                    (*After the French of Georges de Brébeuf*)

Fire, water, woman, are man's ruin,
Says wise Professor Vander Bruin.
By flames a house I hir'd was lost
Last year: and I must pay the cost.
This spring the rains o'erflow'd my ground:
And my best Flanders mare was drown'd.
A slave I am to Clara's eyes:
The gipsy knows her pow'r, and flies.
Fire, water, woman, are my ruin.
And great thy wisdom, Vander Bruin.

IN IMITATION OF ANACREON 208

Let 'em censure: what care I?
The herd of critics I defy.
Let the wretches know, I write
Regardless of their grace, or spite.
No, no: the fair, the gay, the young
Govern the numbers of my song.
All that they approve is sweet:
And all is sense, that they repeat.

Bid the warbling Nine retire:
Venus, string thy servant's lyre:
Love shall be my endless theme:
Pleasure shall triumph over fame:
And when these maxims I decline,
Apollo, may thy fate be mine:
May I grasp at empty praise;
And lose the nymph, to gain the bays.

When Bibo thought fit from the world to retreat,
As full of champagne as an egg's full of meat,
He wak'd in the boat, and to Charon he said,
He would be set back for he was not yet dead:
Trim the boat and sit quiet, stern Charon replied,
You may have forgot, you was drunk when you died.

210   *QUID SIT FUTURUM CRAS FUGE QUÆRERE* ★

For what to-morrow shall disclose,
May spoil what you to-night propose:
England may change; or Chloe stray:
Love and life are for to-day.

211   EPITAPH
          ⟨on Francis Atterbury, Bishop of Rochester⟩

Meek Francis lies here, friend, without stop or stay,
As you value your peace, make the best of your way.
Tho' arrested at present by Death's caitiff claw,
If he stirs, he may yet have recourse to the law:
And in the King's Bench should a verdict be found
That by livery and seisin his grave is his ground,
He may claim to himself what is strictly his due,
And an action of trespass will straitway ensue,
That you without right on his premises tread,
On a single surmise that the owner is dead.

★ Avoid asking what to-morrow may bring. (Horace, *Odes* I.IX.13).

Gilbertus Glanvil, whose heart was as hard as an anvil,
Always litigious when he should have been highly religious,
Still charg'd with lawsuits he to that court aptly descended
Where quiet appears not and quarrels never are ended.

AN EPITAPH　213

Stet quicunque volet potens
Aulae culmine lubrico, etc. Senec.★

Interr'd beneath this marble stone
Lie Saunt'ring J A C K, and Idle J O A N,
While rolling threescore years and one
Did round this globe their courses run;
If human things went ill or well;
If changing empires rose or fell;
The morning past, the evening came,
And found this couple still the same.
They walk'd and eat, good folks: What then?
Why then they walk'd and eat again:
They soundly slept the night away:
They did just nothing all the day:
And having buried children four,
Would not take pains to try for more.
Nor sister either had, nor brother:
They seem'd just tallied for each other.

　Their moral and economy
Most perfectly they made agree:

★ See Notes.

Each virtue kept its proper bound,
Nor trespass'd on the other's ground.
Nor fame, nor censure they regarded:
They neither punish'd, nor rewarded.
He car'd not what the footmen did:
Her maids she neither prais'd, nor chid:
So ev'ry servant took his course;
And bad at first, they all grew worse.
Slothful disorder fill'd his stable;
And sluttish plenty deck'd her table.
Their beer was strong; their wine was port;
Their meal was large; their grace was short.
They gave the poor the remnant-meat,
Just when it grew not fit to eat.

They paid the church and parish rate;
And took, but read not the receipt:
For which they claim'd their Sunday's due,
Of slumb'ring in an upper pew.

No man's defects sought they to know;
So never made themselves a foe.
No man's good deeds did they commend;
So never rais'd themselves a friend.

Nor cherish'd they relations poor:
That might decrease their present store:
Nor barn nor house did they repair:
That might oblige their future heir.

They neither added, nor confounded:
They neither wanted, nor abounded.
Each Christmas they accompts did clear;
And wound their bottom round the year.
Nor tear, nor smile did they imploy
At news of public grief, or joy.

When bells were rung, and bonfires made,
If ask'd, they ne'er denied their aid:
Their jug was to the ringers carried.
Whoever either died, or married.
Their billet at the fire was found,
Whoever was depos'd, or crown'd.

Nor good, nor bad, nor fools, nor wise,
They would not learn, nor could advise:
Without love, hatred, joy, or fear,
They led—a kind of—as it were:
Nor wish'd, nor car'd, nor laugh'd, nor cried:
And so they liv'd; and so they died.

THE WOMAN'S WISH 214

When Eve did with the snake dispute
    O had they both been dumb,
The apple, of all sin the root,
    O had it been a plum!
And Adam, when thou eat'st the fruit
    O had thou suck'd thy thumb!

A TRUE MAID 215

No, no; for my virginity,
    When I lose that, says Rose, I'll die:
Behind the elms, last night, cried Dick,
    Rose, were you not extremely sick?

Ten months after Florimel happen'd to wed,
And was brought in a laudable manner to bed,
She warbl'd her groans with so charming a voice,
That one half of the parish was stunn'd with the noise.
But when Florimel deign'd to lie privately in,
Ten months before she and her spouse were a-kin,
She chose with such prudence her pangs to conceal,
That her nurse, nay her midwife, scarce heard her once squeal.
Learn, husbands, from hence, for the peace of your lives,
That maids make not half such a tumult, as wives.

(Both from the French of Jacques de Cailly)

217   WRITTEN IN AN OVID

Ovid is the surest guide
    You can name, to show the way
To any woman, maid or bride,
    Who resolves to go astray.

(After the French of Gabriel Gilbert)

218   EPIGRAM

To John I ow'd great obligation;
    But John, unhappily, thought fit
To publish it to all the nation:
    So John and I are more than quit.

(After the French of Jean Ogier de Gombauld)

Tom's sickness did his morals mend;
   His health impair'd, his mind grew stronger.
Bad his beginning, good his end:
   He died when he could live no longer.

EPIGRAM   220

Thy nags (the leanest things alive)
So very hard thou lov'st to drive,
I heard thy anxious coachman say,
It costs thee more in whips than hay.

(From the French of Antoine le Brun)

THE LADY WHO OFFERS HER   221
LOOKING-GLASS TO VENUS*

Venus, take my votive glass:
   Since I am not what I was;
What from this day I shall be,
   Venus, let me never see.

(From the Greek of Plato)

* For earlier and later versions see Nos. 70 and 570

I

I sent for Radcliffe, was so ill
    That other doctors gave me over,
He felt my pulse, prescribed his pill
    And I was likely to recover.

II

But when the wit began to wheeze,
    And wine had warmed the politician,
Cured yesterday of my disease,
    I died last night of my physician.

223   FOR HIS OWN EPITAPH

As doctors give physic by way of prevention,
    Matt alive and in health of his tombstone took care;
For delays are unsafe, and his pious intention
    Might haply be never fulfill'd by his heir.

Then take Matt's word for it, the sculptor is paid,
    That the figure is fine pray believe your own eye,
Yet credit but lightly what more may be said,
    For we flatter ourselves, and teach marble to lie.

Yet counting as far as to fifty his years,
    His virtues and vices were as other men's are,
High hopes he conceiv'd, and he smother'd great fears,
    In a life party-colour'd, half pleasure half care.

Nor to business a drudge, nor to faction a slave,
    He strove to make int'rest and freedom agree.
In public employments industrious and grave,
    And alone with his friends, how merry was he.

Now in equipage stately, now humbly on foot,
    Both fortunes he tried but to neither would trust,
And whirl'd in the round, as the wheel turn'd about
    He found riches had wings, and knew man was but dust.

This verse little polish'd tho' mighty sincere
    Sets neither his titles nor merit to view,
It says that his relics collected lie here,
    And no mortal yet knows too if this may be true.

Fierce robbers there are that infest the highway,
    So Matt may be kill'd and his bones never found;
False witness at court, and fierce tempests at sea,
    So Matt may yet chance to be hang'd, or be drown'd.

If his bones lie in earth, roll in sea, fly in air,
    To fate we must yield, and the things are the same,
And if passing thou giv'st him a smile, or a tear,
    He cares not—yet prythee be kind to his fame.

⟨ON HIMSELF⟩   224

        Nobles, and heralds by your leave,
        Here lies what once was Matthew Prior,
        The son of Adam and of Eve,
        Can Stuart, or Nassau go higher.

HUMAN LIFE   225

    What trifling coil do we poor mortals keep;
    Wake, eat, and drink, evacuate, and sleep.

Yes, every poet is a fool:
  By demonstration Ned can show it:
Happy, could Ned's inverted rule
  Prove every fool to be a poet.

(After the French of Scévole de Sainte-Marthe)

227 ANOTHER VERSION, BY
ALEXANDER POPE
1688–1744

Sir, I admit your gen'ral rule
That every poet is a fool:
But you yourself may serve to show it,
That every fool is not a poet.

ANONYMOUS
228 ON MR. HEARNE, THE GREAT ANTIQUARY

Pox on't, says Time to Thomas Hearne,
Whatever I forget, you learn.

229 SAMPSON IMITATED

Jack, eating rotten cheese, did say,
Like Sampson, I my thousands slay:
I vow, quoth Roger, so you do,
And with the self-same weapon too.

Here lies my poor wife, without bed or blanket;   230
But dead as a door nail; God be thanked.

ON A SHREW   231

Here lies my poor wife, much lamented,
She is happy and I am contented.

While Adam slept, from him his Eve arose: 232
Strange! his first sleep should be his last repose.

(After the German of Johann von Besser)

GEORGE GRANVILLE, LORD LANSDOWNE
1667–1735
CLOE   233

Bright as the day, and like the morning fair,
Such Cloe is, and common as the air.

ANONYMOUS
Here lies the great. False marble, where?   234
Nothing but small and sordid dust lies there.

JOHN ARBUTHNOT
1667–1735

235   EPITAPH ON COLONEL FRANCIS CHARTRES

HERE continueth to rot
The body of FRANCIS CHARTRES;
Who, with an INFLEXIBLE CONSTANCY and IMI-
MITABLE UNIFORMITY of life, PERSISTED,
In spite of AGE and INFIRMITIES,
In the practice of EVERY HUMAN VICE,
Excepting PRODIGALITY and HYPOCRISY:
His insatiable AVARICE exempted him from the first,
His matchless IMPUDENCE from the second.

Nor was he more singular in the undeviating *pravity*
of his manners, than successful in *accumulating*
WEALTH:

For, without TRADE or PROFESSION,
Without TRUST of PUBLICK MONEY,
And without BRIBE-WORTHY SERVICE,
He acquired, or more properly created,
A MINISTERIAL ESTATE.

He was the only person of his time
Who cou'd CHEAT without the mask of HONESTY,
Retain his primeval MEANNESS when Possess'd of
TEN THOUSAND a year;
And, having daily deserv'd the GIBBET for what he
did,
Was at last condemn'd to it for what he *could* not *do*.

O indignant reader!
Think not his life useless to mankind!
PROVIDENCE conniv'd at his execrable designs,

84

To give to after-ages a conspicuous PROOF and
    EXAMPLE
Of how small estimation is EXORBITANT WEALTH
    in the sight of GOD, by his bestowing it on the
    most UNWORTHY of ALL MORTALS.

ANONYMOUS

If true that notion, which but few contest,   236
That, in the way of wit, short things are best,
Then in good epigrams two virtues meet,
For 'tis their glory to be short, and sweet.

JONATHAN SWIFT
1667–1745
EPIGRAM   237

As Thomas was cudgell'd one day by his wife,
He took to the street, and fled for his life;
Tom's three dearest friends came by in the squabble,
And sav'd him at once from the shrew and the rabble;
Then ventur'd to give him some sober advice—
But, Tom is a person of honour so nice,
Too wise to take counsel, too proud to take warning,
That he sent to all three a challenge next morning:
Three duels he fought, thrice ventur'd his life;
Went home, and was cudgell'd again by his wife.

ON A WINDOW AT THE FOUR CROSSES.
IN THE WATLING-STREET ROAD,
WARWICKSHIRE

Fool, to put up four crosses at your door,
Put up your wife, she's crosser than all four.

239   THE PLACE OF THE DAMN'D

All folks, who pretend to religion and grace,
Allow there's a Hell, but dispute of the place;
But, if Hell may by logical rules be defin'd
The Place of the Damn'd,—I'll tell you my mind.

Wherever the Damn'd do chiefly abound,
Most certainly there is Hell to be found;
Damn'd poets, Damn'd critics, Damn'd blockheads, Damn'd
        knaves,
Damn'd senators brib'd, Damn's prostitute slaves;
Damn'd lawyers and judges, Damn'd lords and Damn'd squires,
Damn'd spies and informers, Damn'd friends and Damn'd liars;
Damn'd villains corrupted in every station;
Damn'd time-serving priests all over the nation.
And into the bargain, I'll readily give ye,
Damn'd ignorant prelates, and councillors privy.
Then let us no longer by parsons be flamm'd,
For we know by these marks, The Place of the Damn'd:
And Hell to be sure is at Paris or Rome,
How happy for us, that it is not at home!

Here, five feet deep, lies on his back
A cobbler, star-monger, and quack;
Who, to the stars in pure good will,
Does to his best look upward still.
Weep, all you customers, that use
His pills, his almanacs, or shoes:
And you, that did your fortunes seek,
Step to his grave but once a week:
This earth, which bears his body's print,
You'll find has so much virtue in't,
That I durst pawn my ears, 'twill tell
Whate'er concerns you full as well,
In physic, stolen goods, or love,
As he himself could, when above.

THE POWER OF TIME   241

If neither brass, nor marble, can withstand
The mortal force of Time's destructive hand;
If mountains sink to vales, if cities die,
And less'ning rivers mourn their fountains dry;
When my old cassock, said a Welsh divine,
Is out at elbows, why should I repine?

ON THE COLLAR OF MRS. DINGLEY'S   242
LAP-DOG

Pray steal me not, I'm Mrs. Dingley's,
Whose heart in this four-footed thing lies.

Great folks are of a finer mould;
Lord! how politely they can scold.
While a coarse English tongue will itch
For *whore* and *rogue*; and *dog* and *bitch*.

244

With favour and fortune fastidiously blest,
He's loud in his laughter and he's coarse in his jest.
Of favour and fortune unmerited vain,
A sharper in trifles, a dupe in the main,
Achieving of nothing, still promising wonders,
By dint of experience improving in blunders;
Oppressing true merit, exalting the base,
And selling his country to purchase his peace;
A jobber of stocks by retailing false news,
A prater at court in the style of the stews;
Of virtue and worth by profession a giber,
Of juries and senates the bully and briber—
Tho I name not the wretch you know who I mean,
'Tis the cur dog of Britain and spaniel of Spain.*

245   ON HIS OWN DEAFNESS

Deaf, giddy, helpless, left alone,
To all my friends a burthen grown,
No more I hear my church's bell,
Than if it rang out for my knell:
At thunder now no more I start,
Than at the rumbling of a cart:
Nay, what's incredible, alack!
I hardly hear a woman's clack.

* The character of Sir Robert Walpole.

HIC DEPOSITVM EST CORPVS
JONATHAN SWIFT, S.T.P.
HVIVS ECCLESIAE CATHEDRALIS
DECANI,
VBI SAEVA INDIGNATIO
VLTERIVS COR LACERARE NEQUIT.
ABI, VIATOR,
ET IMITARE, SI POTERIS,
STRENVVM PRO VIRILI LIBER-
TATIS VINDICEM.
OBIIT ANNO MDCCXLV
MENSIS OCTOBRIS DIE 19
AETATIS ANNO LXXVIII

(Here lies the body of Jonathan Swift, Professor of Holy Theology, Dean of this cathedral church, where savage indignation can tear his heart no longer. Go, traveller, and if you can imitate one who with his utmost strength protected liberty. He died in the year 1745, on the 19th of October, aged seventy-eight.)

JOHN WINSTANLEY
1678?–1750

ON A CERTAIN EFFEMINATE PEER   247

As Nature H——'s clay was blending,
Uncertain what the work would end in,
Whether a female or a male,
A pin dropt in and turn'd the scale.

Florio, one ev'ning, brisk, and gay,
To pass the tedious hours away,
With three young female rakes sat down,
And play'd at whisk for half a crown;
At length (if fame the truth can tell)
To questions and commands they fell:
Florio, says Cloe, let me see
What Delia wears above her knee;
The youth with ready hand obey'd,
And by her garter caught the maid;
She kindled with affected heat
And rising vig'rous from her seat,
As if she thought him monstrous rude,
Flew to her chamber; he pursu'd;
Then flung her softly on the bed;
And now, my lovely girl, he said,
I bar all squeakings, and oh fies!
Go, bar the door, you fool, she cries.

ON A STINGY BEAU

Curio's rich sideboard seldom sees the light,
Clean is his kitchen, his spits are always bright;
His knives, and spoons, all rang'd in even rows,
No hands molest, or fingers discompose;
A curious jack, hung up to please the eye,
For ever still, whose flyers never fly;
His plates unsullied, shining on the shelf,
For Curio dresses nothing—but himself.

⟨ON GEORGE I's GIFT OF BISHOP MOORE'S   250
LIBRARY TO THE UNIVERSITY OF
CAMBRIDGE, AT THE TIME OF THE
JACOBITE RISINGS⟩

The King, observing with judicious eyes,
The state of both his universities,
To Oxford sent a troop of horse, and why?
That learned body wanted loyalty;
To Cambridge books, as very well discerning,
How much that loyal body wanted learning.

A REPLY TO THE ABOVE, BY   251
SIR WILLIAM BROWNE
(1692–1774)

The King to Oxford sent a troop of horse,
For Tories own no argument but force:
With equal skill to Cambridge books he sent,
For Whigs admit no force but argument.

TO THE REVEREND JOSEPH TRAPP, ON THE   252
FIRST VOLUME OF HIS TRANSLATION
OF THE *AENEID*

Keep the commandments, Trapp, and go no further,
For it is written, That thou shalt not murther.

253 ON SIR JOHN VANBRUGH
⟨THE ARCHITECT⟩

Under this stone, Reader, survey
Dead Sir John Vanbrugh's house of clay.
Lie heavy on him, Earth! for he
Laid many heavy loads on thee!

254 AN AUTHOR'S EPITAPH.
WRITTEN BY HIMSELF

Here lies the author of the "Apparition,"
Who died, God wot, but in a poor condition;
If, reader, you would shun his fate,
Nor write, nor preach for Church or State,
Be dull, exceeding dull, and you'll be great.

ANONYMOUS
255 ON DR. EVANS CUTTING DOWN A ROW OF
TREES AT ST. JOHN'S COLLEGE, OXFORD

Indulgent Nature on each kind bestows
A secret instinct to discern its foes:
The goose, a silly bird, avoids the fox;
Lambs fly from wolves; and sailors steer from rocks.
Evans, the gallows as his fate foresees,
And bears the like antipathy to trees.

EPIGRAM   256

Lasses, like nuts at bottom brown,
   Are ripe, and should be sought;
Else of themselves they will fa' down,
   And syn prove good for nought.

JOHN GAY
1688–1732

MY OWN EPITAPH   257

Life is a jest, and all things show it.
I thought so once; but now I know it.

ALEXANDER POPE
1688–1744

EPIGRAM, IN A MAID OF HONOUR'S   258
PRAYER-BOOK

When Israel's daughters mourn'd their past offences,
They dealt in sackcloth, and turn'd cinder-wenches:
But Richmond's fair-ones never spoil their locks,
They use white powder, and wear holland smocks.
O comely church! where females find clean linen
As decent to repent in, as to sin in.

LORD CONINGSBY'S EPITAPH   259

Here lies Lord Coningsby—be civil,
The rest God knows—so does the Devil.

260   You beat your pate, and fancy wit will come:
              Knock as you please, there's nobody at home.

261   EPITAPH ON JAMES MOORE SMYTHE

              Here lies what had not birth, nor shape, nor fame;
              No gentleman! no man! no-thing! no name!
              For Jammie ne'er grew James; and what they call
              More, shrunk to Smith—and Smith's no name at all.
              Yet die thou can'st not, Phantom, oddly fated:
              For how can no-thing be annihilated?
                           Ex nihilo nihil fit.

262   ON J. M. S. GENT

              To prove himself no plagiary, Moore
              Has writ such stuff, as none e'er writ before.
              Thy prudence, Moore, is like that Irish wit,
              Who shew'd his breech, to prove 'twas not beshit.

263   ON AUTHORS AND BOOKSELLERS*

              What authors lose, their booksellers have won,
              So pimps grow rich, while gallants are undone.

264   ON POETS

              Damnation follows death in other men,
              But your damn'd poet lives and writes agen.
                     * i.e. publishers.

Shall royal praise be rhym'd by such a ribald,
As fopling Cibber, or Attorney Tibbald?
Let's rather wait one year for better luck;
One year may make a singing swan of Duck,
Great George! such servants since thou well can'st lack,
Oh! save the salary, and drink the sack!

ON COLLEY CIBBER'S DECLARATION THAT   266
HE WILL HAVE THE LAST WORD WITH
MR. POPE

Quoth Cibber to Pope, tho' in verse you foreclose,
I'll have the last word, for by God I'll write prose.
Poor Colley, thy reas'ning is none of the strongest,
For know, the last word is the word that lasts longest.

Cibber! write all thy verses upon glasses,   267
The only way to save 'em from our arses.

ON DENNIS   268

Should Dennis print how once you robb'd your brother,
Traduc'd your monarch, and debauch'd your mother;
Say what revenge on Dennis can be had;
Too dull for laughter, for reply too mad?
Of one so poor you cannot take the law;
On one so old your sword you cannot draw.
Uncag'd then let the harmless monster rage,
Secure in dullness, madness, want, and age.

269 EPIGRAM. ENGRAVED ON THE COLLAR
OF A DOG WHICH I GAVE TO HIS ROYAL
HIGHNESS

I am his Highness' dog at Kew;
Pray tell me Sir, whose dog are you?

270 EPIGRAM. ON ONE WHO MADE LONG
EPITAPHS

Freind! for your epitaphs I'm griev'd,
Where still so much is said,
One half will never be believ'd,
The other never read.

271 EPITAPH
⟨on Laetitia, three years old⟩

See here, nice Death, to please his palate
Takes a young lettuce for a sallet.

272 EPITAPH. FOR ONE WHO WOULD NOT BE
BURIED IN WESTMINSTER ABBEY

Heroes, and Kings! your distance keep:
In peace let one poor poet sleep,
Who never flatter'd folks like you:
Let Horace blush, and Virgil too.

Under this marble, or under this sill,
Or under this turf, or e'en what they will;
Whatever an heir, or a friend in his stead,
Or any good creature shall lay o'er my head;
Lies he who ne'er car'd, and still cares not a pin,
What they said, or may say of the mortal within.
But who living and dying, serene still and free,
Trusts in God, that as well as he was, he shall be.

⟨ON THE ERECTION OF SHAKESPEARE'S 274
STATUE IN WESTMINSTER ABBEY⟩

After an hundred and thirty years' nap,
Enter Shakespear, with a loud clap.

When other ladies to the Groves go down, 275
Corinna still, and Fulvia stay in town;
These ghosts of Beauty ling'ring here reside,
And haunt the places where their honour died.

TWO OR THREE; OR A RECEIPT 276
TO MAKE A CUCKOLD

Two or three visits, and two or three bows,
Two or three civil things, two or three vows,
Two or three kisses, with two or three sighs,
Two or three Jesus's—and let me dies—
Two or three squeezes, and two or three towses,
With two or three thousand pound lost at their houses,
Can never fail cuckolding two or three spouses.

EPITAPH. INTENDED FOR SIR ISAAC
NEWTON, IN WESTMINSTER ABBEY

ISAACUS NEWTONIUS
Quem Immortalem
Testantur Tempus, Natura, Coelum:
Mortalem
Hoc Marmor fatetur.*

Nature, and Nature's laws lay hid in night.
God said, Let Newton be! and all was light.

278 FOLLOWING THE ABOVE, BY
SIR JOHN SQUIRE
1884–1958

It did not last; the Devil howling *Ho,*
Let Einstein be, restored the status quo.

ALEXANDER POPE 1688–1744 AND
THOMAS PARNELL 1679–1718

279 ON RIDING TO SEE DEAN SWIFT IN THE
MIST OF THE MORNING

How foolish men on expeditions go!
Unweeting wantons of their wetting woe!
For drizzling damps descend adown the plain
And seem a thicker dew, or thinner rain;
Yet dew or rain may wet us to the shift,
We'll not be slow to visit Dr. Swift.

* Isaac Newton, whose immortality Time, Nature and the Heavens declare:
whose death this marble makes known.

A SUMMARY OF LORD LYTTELTON'S *ADVICE*   280

Be plain in dress and sober in your diet;
In short, my deary, kiss me, and be quiet.

EPITAPH
⟨ON THE STANTON HARCOURT LOVERS⟩   281

Here lies John Hughes* and Sarah Drew.
Perhaps you'll say, what's that to you?
Believe me, friend, much may be said
On this poor couple that are dead.
On Sunday next they should have married;
But see how oddly things are carry'd,
On Thursday last it rain'd and lighten'd,
These tender lovers sadly frighten'd
Shelter'd beneath the cocking hay
In hopes to pass the storm away.
But the bold thunder found them out
(Commission'd for that end no doubt)
And seizing on their trembling breath,
Consign'd them to the shades of death.
Who knows if 'twas not kindly done?
For had they seen the next year's sun,
A beaten wife and cuckold swain
Had jointly curs'd the marriage chain.
Now they are happy in their doom,
For P. has wrote upon their tomb.

* Properly Hewet.

ANOTHER ON THE SAME, BY
ALEXANDER POPE
1688–1744

Here lie two poor lovers, who had the mishap
Tho' very chaste people, to die of a clap.

ANONYMOUS
283 SPOKEN BY VENUS ON SEEING HER STATUE
DONE BY PRAXITELES

Anchises, Paris, and Adonis too,
Have seen me naked, and expos'd to view;
All these I freely own, without denying:
But where has this Praxiteles been prying?

(After the Greek)

284   Thy eyes and eyebrows I could spare,
Nor for thy nose do I much care;
I could dispense too with thy teeth,
And with thy lips, and with thy breath,
And with thy breasts, and with thy belly,
And with that which I won't tell ye;
And, to be short—hark, in thy ear,
Faith, I could spare thee all, my dear.

Fair Ursly, in a merry mood,   285
    Consulted her physician,
What time was best to stir the blood,
    And spirits, by coition.

Quoth Woodward, If my judgment's right,
    And answer worth returning,
You'll find it pleasantest o'er night,
    Most wholesome in the morning.

Quoth Ursly, Then, for pleasure's sake,
    Each ev'ning will I take it:
And ev'ry morning, when I wake,
    My constant physic make it.

(After the Latin of Annibal Cruceius)

ON A WINDOW AT AN INN   286

Give me sweet nectar in a kiss,
That I may be replete with bliss.
                                                Strephon

Give me but claret in a glass;
And as for kissing, kiss my arse.
                                                Silenus

ON A DOG-COLLAR   287

At thieves I bark; at lovers wag my tail;
And thus I please both Lord and Lady Thrale.

(After the Latin of Joachim du Bellay)

Since in religion all men disagree
And some one God believe, some thirty and some three;
Since no religion, call'd by any name,
In ten, nay two believers is the same;
But since in Woman, from the days of Eve,
All nations, tongues and languages believe;
Since in this faith no heresies we find,
To love let our religion be resign'd,
And Caelia reign the Goddess of mankind.

289   MALVERN WATERS

The Malvern water, says Dr. John Wall,
Is famed for containing just nothing at all.

JOHN BYROM
1692–1763
290   ⟨TWO MONOPOLISTS⟩

Bone and Skin,
Two millers thin,
Would starve the town, or near it;—
But be it known
To Skin and Bone
That Flesh and Blood can't bear it.

Some say, compar'd to Bononcini
That Mynheer Handel's but a ninny;
Others aver, that he to Handel
Is scarcely fit to hold a candle.
Strange all this difference should be
'Twixt Tweedle-*dum* and Tweedle-*dee*!

TO AN OFFICER IN THE ARMY, INTENDED 292
TO ALLAY THE VIOLENCE OF PARTY SPIRIT

God bless the king—I mean the faith's defender;
God bless—(no harm in blessing)—the pretender;
But who pretender is, or who is king,
God bless us all—that's quite another thing.

MESSENGER MOUNSEY
1693–1788

ON THE PHYSICIAN TO CHELSEA 293
HOSPITAL BY HIMSELF

Here lie my old bones: my vexation now ends:
I have lived much too long for myself and my friends.
As to churches and churchyards, which man may call holy,
'Tis a rank piece of witchcraft, and founded in folly.
What the next world may be, never troubled my pate;
And be what it may, I beseech you, O Fate!
When the bodies of millions rise up in a riot,
To let the old carcase of Mounsey be quiet.

SIR HILDEBRAND JACOB
1693–1739

294   ON DELIA

Here Delia's buried at fourscore:
When young, a lewd, rapacious whore,
Vain, and expensive; but when old,
A pious, sordid, drunken scold.

295   SENT TO HIM, AS HE WHISPER'D ****

Swain, give o'er your fond pretension,
Wit's above her apprehension;
        'Tis no merit to excel.
Any powder'd thing in breeches,
Who can make soft, simple speeches
        Pleases Myra full as well.

PHILIP DORMER STANHOPE, EARL OF CHESTERFIELD
1694–1773

296   IMPROMPTU LINES ON BEING ASKED BY
        SIR THOMAS ROBINSON, SURNAMED THE
        LONG, TO WRITE SOME VERSES ON HIMSELF

Unlike my subject now shall be my song,
It shall be witty, and it shan't be long.

In Flavia's eyes is every grace,
  She's handsome as she could be;
With Jacob's beauty in her face,
  And Esau's where it should be.

ANONYMOUS REPLY TO THE ABOVE   298

Flavia's a name a deal too free
  With holy writ to blend her;
Henceforth let Nell Susanna be,
  And Chesterfield the Elder.

ANONYMOUS
FROM *EPIGRAMS IN DISTICH*,   299
1740

I
THE FINE LADY REFORM'D
She talks not, plays not, visits not, in bed
Eats not, frequents no plays, no balls:—she's dead.

II
TO A FLATTERER
Should I believe you, e'en my oaths are witty:
And when I fart, nothing can be more pretty.

III
THE PURSE-PROUD
Will to be tickled wants; has got the itch:
Calls himself poor, that we may call him rich.

IV
A VAIN MAN RUINING IN DEBT
See columns rang'd in proud Palladian style!
And its lord's fortune finish'd with the pile!

WILLIAM OLDYS
1696–1761

300   ON HIMSELF

In word and Will I am a friend to you;
And one friend Old is worth a hundred new.

SAMUEL JOHNSON
1709–1784

301   À SON LIT

In bed we laugh, in bed we cry,
And born in bed, in bed we die;
The near approach a bed may shew
Of human bliss to human woe.

(*From the French of Isaac de Benserade*)

If at your coming princes disappear,
Comets! come every day—and stay a year.

(From the Italian)

LINES ON THOMAS WARTON'S POEMS 303

I

Wheresoe'er I turn my view,
All is strange, yet nothing new;
Endless labour all along,
Endless labour to be wrong;
Phrase that Time has flung away,
Uncouth words in disarray:
Trickt in antique ruff and bonnet,
Ode and elegy and sonnet.

II

Hermit hoar, in solemn cell,
   Wearing out life's evening gray;
Smite thy bosom, sage, and tell,
   Where is bliss, and which the way?

Thus I spake; and speaking sigh'd;
   Scarce repress'd the starting tear;—
When the smiling sage reply'd—
   Come, my lad, and drink some beer.

To robbers furious, and to lovers tame,
I pleas'd my master, and I pleas'd my dame.

(After the Latin of Joachim du Bellay)

305   TO MRS THRALE ON HER THIRTY-FIFTH
BIRTHDAY

Oft in danger yet alive
We are come to Thirty-five;
Long may better years arrive,
Better years than Thirty-five;
Could philosophers contrive
Life to stop at Thirty-five,
Time his hours should never drive
O'er the bounds of Thirty-five:
High to soar and deep to dive
Nature gives at Thirty-five;
Ladies—stock and tend your hive,
Trifle not at Thirty-five:
For howe'er we boast and strive,
Life declines from Thirty-five;
He that ever hopes to thrive
Must begin by Thirty-five:
And those who wisely wish to wive
Must look on Thrale at Thirty-five.

★ For another version, see No. 287.

DOCTOR JOHNSON   306

Here lies poor Johnson. Reader! have a care,
Tread lightly, lest you rouse a sleeping bear.
Religious, moral, gen'rous and humane,
He was, but self-conceited, rude, and vain:
Ill-bred, and overbearing in dispute,
A scholar and a Christian, yet a brute.
Would you know all his wisdom and his folly,
His actions, sayings, mirth, and melancholy,
Boswell and Thrale, retailers of his wit,
Will tell you how he wrote, and talk'd, and spit.

ANONYMOUS

AN EPITAPH ON WILLIAM WHITEHEAD   307
INTENDED FOR HIS MONUMENT IN
WESTMINSTER ABBEY

Beneath this stone a Poet Laureate lies,
Nor great, nor good, nor foolish, nor yet wise;
Not meanly humble, nor yet swell'd with pride,
He simply liv'd—and just as simply died:
Each year his Muse produc'd a Birth-Day Ode,
Compos'd with flattery in the usual mode:
For this, and but for this, to George's praise,
The Bard was pension'd and receiv'd the bays.

Pride is his pity, artifice his praise
A mask his virtue, and his fame a blaze;
Insult his charity, his friendship fear,
And nothing but his vanity, sincere.

309　　　　　ON HIMSELF

Here lies Piron—a man of no position,
Who was not even an Academician.

(From the French of Alexis Piron)

WILLIAM SHENSTONE
1714–1763

310　　ON THE CLERK OF A COUNTRY PARISH

Here lies, within his tomb, so calm,
　　Old Giles: Pray sound his knell;
Who thought no song was like a psalm,
　　No music like a bell.

THOMAS GRAY
1716–1771

311　　　ON DR. KEENE, BISHOP OF CHESTER

The Bishop of Chester
Though wiser than Nestor
And fairer than Esther,
If you scratch him will fester.

EPITAPH ON DR. KEENE

⟨who married a rich draper's daughter⟩

Here lies Dr. Keene, the good Bishop of Chester,
Who eat up a fat goose, but could not digest her.

EPITAPH ON DR. KEENE'S WIFE

Here lies Mistress Keene the Bishop of Chester,
She had a bad face, which did always molest her.

⟨FOR THE PORTRAIT OF A MEDDLING IMPUDENT CLERIC⟩

Such Tophet was; so looked the grinning fiend
Whom many a frightened prelate called his friend;
I saw them bow and, while they wished him dead,
With servile simper nod the mitred head.
Our Mother-Church with half-averted sight
Blushed as she blessed her grisly proselyte:
Hosannahs rung through Hell's tremendous borders,
And Satan's self had thoughts of taking orders.

DAVID GARRICK
1716–1779

315   UPON A CERTAIN LORD'S GIVING SOME
       THOUSAND POUNDS FOR A HOUSE

So many thousands for a house!
For you, of all the world, Lord Mouse!
A little house would best accord
With you, my very little lord!
And then exactly match'd would be
Your house and hospitality.

316   AN EPIGRAM UPON A YOUNG GENTLEMAN
       REFUSING TO WALK WITH THE AUTHOR
       IN THE PARK, BECAUSE HE WAS NOT
       DRESS'D WELL

Friend Col and I, both full of whim,
    To shun each other oft agree;
For I'm not beau enough for him,
    And he's too much a beau for me.
Then let us from each other fly,
    And arm in arm no more appear;
That I may ne'er offend your eye,
    That you may ne'er offend my ear.

317   EPITAPH ON LAURENCE STERNE

Shall pride a heap of sculptur'd marble raise,
Some worthless, unmourn'd titled fool to praise;
And shall we not by one poor gravestone learn
Where genius, wit, and humour sleep with Sterne?

> For physic and farces,
> His equal there scarce is;
> His farces are physic,
> His physic a farce is.

ON OLIVER GOLDSMITH   319

Here lies Nolly Goldsmith, for shortness call'd Noll,
Who wrote like an angel, but talk'd like poor Poll.

ANONYMOUS
ON A NEW DUKE   320

> You ask why gold and velvet bind
>   The temples of that cringing thief?
> Is it so strange a thing to find
>   A toad below a strawberry leaf?

WRITTEN ON A LOOKING-GLASS   321

> I change, and so do women too;
> But I reflect—which women never do.

'Tis bad enough, in man or woman,
To steal a goose from off a common;
But surely he's without excuse
Who steals the common from the goose.

323   IN MEMORY OF CAPTAIN UNDERWOOD,
WHO WAS DROWNED

Here lies free from blood and slaughter
Once Underwood—now under water.

324   GRIZZEL GRIMME

Here lies with Death auld Grizzel Grimme,
    Lincluden's ugly witch;
O Death, how horrid is thy taste
    To bed with such a bitch!

HORACE WALPOLE
1717–1797

325   All praise your face, your verses none abuse,
Yet think you buy your face, and hire your muse.

(After the French)

Your pinks, your tulips live an hour;
A fortnight binds your utmost power.
Flora, the niggard goddess, pays
With short-liv'd joys the toll of days.
But, Walter Clark, your happy lot
Is fallen in a fairer spot:
A Muse has deign'd to view your bower,
And stamp'd immortal every flower.
Her breath new perfumes can disclose,
Her touch improve the damask rose;
And ages hence the buds you raise
Shall bloom in Nuneham's living rays.
The lilies of the field, that shone
With brighter blaze than Solomon,
Shall beg to quit their rural stations
And mix with Walter Clark's carnations.

ON THE TRANSLATION OF ANACREON   327

On gay Anacreon's joy-inspiring line
Pour'd all his juice the glowing god of wine,
But in the poet's bowl his tame translator
Has mix'd such suffocating draughts of water,
That yawn to yawn and nod to nod succeeds
And Drunkenness grows sober as she reads.

An estate and an earldom at seventy-four!
Had I sought them or wish'd them, 'twould add one fear more,
That of making a countess when almost four-score.
But Fortune, who scatters her gifts out of season,
Though unkind to my limbs, has still left me my reason;
And whether she lowers or lifts me, I'll try
In the same simple style I have liv'd in, to die;
For ambition too humble, for meanness too high.

329   EPITAPHS ON TWO PIPING-BULLFINCHES
OF LADY OSSORY'S, BURIED UNDER A
ROSE-BUSH IN HER GARDEN

I

All flesh is grass, and so are feathers too:
Beneath a damask rose, in good old age,
Here lies the tenant of a noble cage.
For forty moons he charm'd his lady's ear,
And pip'd obedient oft as she drew near,
Though now stretch'd out upon a clay-cold bier.
But when the last shrill flageolet shall sound,
And raise all dickybirds from holy ground,
His little corpse again its wings shall plume,
And sing eternally the self-same tune
From everlasting night to everlasting noon.

II

ON THE OTHER BULLFINCH, BURIED IN THE
SAME PLACE

Beneath the same bush rests his brother—
What serves for one will serve for t'other.

★ Epitaph of the living Author.

HENRY HARINGTON
1727–1816

THE ABBEY CHURCH AT BATH   330

These walls, so full of monument and bust,
Show how Bath-waters serve to lay the dust.

THOMAS WARTON
1728–1790

ON LEANDER'S SWIMMING OVER THE   331
HELLESPONT TO HERO

When bold Leander sought his distant fair,
(Nor could the sea a braver burthen bear)
Thus to the swelling wave he spoke his woe,
Drown me on my return—but spare me as I go.

(After the Latin of Martial)

OLIVER GOLDSMITH
1728–1774

⟨ON EDMUND BURKE⟩   332

Here lies our good Edmund, whose genius was such,
We scarcely can praise it or blame it too much;
Who, born for the universe, narrowed his mind,
And to party gave up what was meant for mankind;
Though fraught with all learning, yet straining his throat
To persuade Tommy Townshend to lend him a vote;
Who, too deep for his hearers, still went on refining,
And thought of convincing, while they thought of dining;
Though equal to all things, for all things unfit;

Too nice for a statesman, too proud for a wit;
For a patriot, too cool; for a drudge, disobedient;
And too fond of the *right* to pursue the *expedient*;
In short, 'twas his fate, unemployed or in place, sir,
To eat mutton cold and cut blocks with a razor.

333   ⟨ON SIR JOSHUA REYNOLDS⟩

   Here Reynolds is laid and, to tell you my mind,
He has not left a better or wiser behind:
His pencil was striking, resistless and grand;
His manners were gentle, complying and bland;
Still born to improve us in every part,
His pencil our faces, his manners our heart;
To coxcombs averse, yet most civilly steering,
When they judged without skill he was still hard of hearing;
When they talked of their Raphaels, Correggios and stuff,
He shifted his trumpet and only took snuff.

JOHN CUNNINGHAM
1729–1773

334   AN EPIGRAM

            A member of the modern great
                Pass'd Sawney with his budget,
            The peer was in a car of state,
                The tinker forc'd to trudge it.

            But Sawney shall receive the praise
                His Lordship would parade for:
            One's debtor for his dappled greys,
                And t'other's shoes are paid for.

That he was born it cannot be denied;
He ate, drank, slept, talk'd politics, and died.

(After the Greek of Simonides)

ANONYMOUS

Here lies the body of Richard Hind,   336
Who was neither ingenious, sober, nor kind.

JOHNNY DOO   337

Wha lies here?
I, Johnny Doo.
Hoo, Johnny, is that you?
Ay, man, but a'm dead noo.

ON SIR JOHN GUISE   338

Here lies the body of Sir John Guise,
Nobody laughs, and nobody cries;
Where his soul is, and how it fares,
Nobody knows, and nobody cares.

DANIEL SAUL   339

Here lies the body of Daniel Saul,
Spitalfields weaver, and that's all.

* For an Elizabethan version see No. 57.

340   Here lies I, no wonder I'm dead,
               For a broad-wheel'd waggon went over my head.

WILLIAM COWPER
1731–1800

341   PRUDENT SIMPLICITY

That thou mayst injure no man, dove-like be,
And serpent-like, that none may injure thee!

(After the Latin of John Owen)

342   AN EPITAPH★

My name—my country—what are they to thee?
What—whether base or proud, my pedigree?
Perhaps I far surpass'd all other men—
Perhaps I fell below them all—what then?
Suffice it, stranger! that thou seest a tomb—
Thou know'st its use—it hides—no matter whom.

(After the Greek of Paulos)

SIR WILLIAM JONES
1746–1794

343   A MORAL TETRASTICH FROM THE PERSIAN

On parent knees, a naked new-born child,
Weeping thou satst, when all around thee smil'd;
So live, that, sinking in thy last long sleep,
Calm thou mayst smile, when all around thee weep.

★ For another version see No. 457.

THOMAS, LORD ERSKINE
1750–1823

⟨ON TOM MOORE'S TRANSLATION OF   344
ANACREON⟩

Oh! mourn not for Anacreon dead;
Oh! weep not for Anacreon fled;
The lyre still breathes he touch'd before,
For we have one Anacreon Moore.

⟨ON A JUDGE FROM SCOTLAND⟩   345

James Alan Park
Came naked stark,
From Scotland,
And now wears clothes
And lives with beaux,
In England.

RICHARD BRINSLEY SHERIDAN
1751–1816

CLIO'S PROTEST   346

You write with ease, to shew your breeding;
But easy writing's vile hard reading.

ON LADY ANNE HAMILTON   347

Pray how did she look? Was she pale, was she wan?
She was blooming and red as a cherry—poor Anne.

Did she eat? Did she drink? Yes, she drank up a can,
And ate very near a whole partridge—poor Anne.

Pray what did she do? Why, she talked to each man
And flirted with Morpeth and Breanbie—poor Anne.

Pray how was she drest? With a turban and fan,
With ear-rings, with chains, and with bracelets—poor Anne.

And how went she home? In a good warm sedan
With a muff and a cloak and a tippet—poor Anne.

JOSEPH JEKYLL
1752–1837

348   See, one physician, like a sculler, plies,
The patient lingers and by inches dies.
But two physicians, like a pair of oars,
Waft him more swiftly to the Stygian shores.

WILLIAM LORT MANSEL
1753–1820

349   ⟨A STANZA COMPLETED⟩

The sun's perpendicular rays
Illumine the depth of the sea—
The fishes beginning to sweat,
Cried "Damn it, how hot we shall be!"

THOMAS ROWLANDSON?
1757–1827

⟨EPITAPH ON A WILLING GIRL⟩   350

Here lies intombed
    Beneath these bricks
The scabbard of ten
    Thousand pricks.

WILLIAM BLAKE
1757–1827

O Lapwing, thou fliest around the heath,   351
Nor see'st the net that is spread beneath.
Why dost thou not fly among the corn fields?
They cannot spread nets where a harvest yields.

The sword sang on the barren heath,   352
    The sickle in the fruitful field;
The sword he sung a song of death,
    But could not make the sickle yield.

When Sir Joshua Reynolds died   353
All Nature was degraded;
The King dropp'd a tear into the Queen's ear,
And all his pictures faded.

Give pensions to the Learned Pig   354
    Or the Hare playing on a Tabor;
Anglus can never see perfection
But in the journeyman's labour.

Fortune favours the brave, old proverbs say;
But not with money: that is not the way.
Turn back, turn back: you travel all in vain.
Turn thro' the iron gate down Sneaking Lane.

356

A pretty sneaking knave I knew—
O Mr. Cromek, how do ye do?

357

TO HAYLEY

Your friendship oft has made my heart to ache:
Do be my enemy for friendship's sake.

358

To forgive enemies Hayley does pretend,
Who never in his life forgave a friend.

359

AN EPITAPH

I was buried near this dyke,
That my friends may weep as much as they like.

360

ANOTHER

Here lies John Trot, the friend of all mankind:
He has not left one enemy behind.
Friends were quite hard to find, old authors say;
But now they stand in every bodies way.

I mock thee not, tho' I by thee am mocked.
   Thou call'st me madman, but I call thee blockhead.

When a man has married a wife, he finds out whether   362
Her knees and elbows are only glued together.

     Abstinence sows sand all over   363
     The ruddy limbs and flaming hair,
     But Desire Gratified
     Plants fruits of life and beauty there.

   THE QUESTION ANSWER'D   364

     What is it men in women do require?
     The lineaments of gratified desire.
     What is it women do in men require?
     The lineaments of gratified desire.

Her whole life is an epigram, smart, smooth, and neatly penn'd,   365
Platted quite neat to catch applause with a sliding noose at the
   end.

     Grown old in love from seven till seven times seven,   366
     I oft have wish'd for Hell for ease from Heaven.

He who binds himself to a joy
Does the winged life destroy;
But he who kisses the joy as it flies
Lives in eternity's sun rise.

368   AN ANSWER TO THE PARSON

"Why of the sheep do you not learn peace?"
"Because I don't want you to shear my fleece."

?JULIUS CAESAR IBBETSON
1759–1817

369   O mortal man, that lives by bread,
What is it makes thy nose so red?
Thou silly fool, that look'st so pale,
'Tis drinking Sally Birkett's ale.

RICHARD PORSON
1759–1808

370   ⟨ON A GERMAN SCHOLAR⟩

The Germans, in Greek,
Are sadly to seek;
Not five in five score,
But ninety-five more,—
All, save only Hermann,
And Hermann's a German.

Miss Seward:
Tuneful poet, Britain's glory,
  Mr. Hayley, that is you.

Hayley:
Ma'am, you carry all before you,
  Trust me, Lichfield Swan, you do.

Miss Seward:
Ode, didactic, epic, sonnet,
  Mr. Hayley, you're divine.

Hayley:
Ma'am, I'll take my oath upon it,
  You yourself are all the Nine.

⟨ON LATIN GERUNDS⟩   372

When Dido found Aeneas would not come,
She mourn'd in silence, and was *Di-do-dum*.

THE BATHOS   373

"Since mountains sink to vales, and valleys die,
"And seas and rivers mourn their sources dry;
"When my old cassock," says a Welsh divine,
"Is out at elbows, why should I repine?"

I went to Frankfort and got drunk
With that most learned professor, Brunck;
I went to Worts and got more drunken
With that more learned professor, Ruhnken.

375   ⟨ON A FELLOW OF TRINITY COLLEGE,
CAMBRIDGE⟩

Here lies a Doctor of Divinity;
    He was a Fellow too of Trinity:
He knew as much about Divinity,
    As other Fellows do of Trinity.

ROBERT BURNS
1759–1796

376   ON A SCHOOLMASTER IN CLEISH PARISH,
FIFESHIRE

Here lie Willie M--hie's banes,
    O Satan, when ye tak him,
Gie him the schulin' o' your weans;
    For clever Deils he'll mak 'em.

377   GRACE AFTER DINNER

O Lord, since we have feasted thus,
    Which we so little merit,
Let Meg now take away the flesh,
    And Jock bring in the spirit!
                        Amen

No more of your titled acquaintances boast,
    Nor of the gay groups you have seen;
A crab louse is but a crab louse at last,
    Tho' stack to the cunt of a Queen.

378

⟨EPITAPH⟩

379

Lo worms enjoy the seat of bliss
Where Lords and Lairds afore did kiss.

⟨EPITAPH FOR WILLIAM NICOL⟩

380

Ye maggots, feed on Willie's brains,
    For few sic feasts ye've gotten;
An' fix your claws into his heart,
    For fient a bit o't's rotten.

ON LORD GALLOWAY

381

No Stewart art thou, Galloway,
    The Stewarts all were brave;
Besides, the Stewarts were but fools,
    Not one of them a knave.

ON A NOISY POLEMIC

382

Below thir stanes lie Jamie's banes;
    O Death, it's my opinion,
Thou ne'er took such a bleth'ran bitch
    Into thy dark dominion!

383   A head pure, sinless quite of brain or soul,
       The very image of a Barber's Pole;
       Just shews a human face and wears a wig,
       And looks when well-friseur'd, amazing big.

384   Here cursing swearing Burton lies,
               A buck, a beau, or *Dem my eyes*!
           Who in his life did little good,
               And his last words were, *Dem my blood*!

385   ON W. R-----, ESQ.

       So vile was poor Wat, such a miscreant slave,
       That the worms even damn'd him when laid in his grave.
       "In his scull there is famine" a starv'd reptile cries;
       "And his heart it is poison!" another replies.

386   THE BOOK-WORMS

           Through and through the inspired leaves,
               Ye maggots, make your windings;
           But, oh! respect his lordship's taste,
               And spare his golden bindings.

387   TO MR. E---- ON HIS TRANSLATION OF
           AND COMMENTARIES ON MARTIAL

           O thou, whom Poesy abhors,
           Whom Prose has turned out of doors,
           Heard'st thou yon groan?—proceed no further!
           'Twas laurell'd Martial calling, Murther!

Pray Billy Pitt explain thy rigs,
    This new poll-tax of thine!
"I mean to mark the Guinea pigs
    From other common Swine."

⟨THE KEEKIN' GLASS⟩ 389

How daur ye ca' me "Howlet-face,"
    Ye blear-e'ed, wither'd spectre?
Ye only spied the keekin' glass,
    An' there ye saw your picture.

GEORGE COLMAN
1762–1836

ON SIR NATHANIEL WRAXALL 390
THE HISTORIAN

Misplacing—mistaking—
Misquoting—misdating—
Men, manners, things, facts all,
Here lies Nathan Wraxall.

SAMUEL ROGERS
1763–1855

AN EPITAPH 391
ON A ROBIN-REDBREAST

Tread lightly here, for here, 'tis said,
When piping winds are hushed around,

A small voice wakes from underground,
Where now his tiny bones are laid.
No more in lone and leafless groves,
With ruffled wing and faded breast,
His friendless, homeless spirit roves;
—Gone to the world where birds are blest!
Where never cat glides o'er the green,
Or school-boy's giant form is seen;
But Love, and Joy, and smiling Spring
Inspire their little souls to sing!

392   ⟨ON JOHN WILLIAM WARD M.P.⟩

Ward has no heart, they say; but I deny it;—
He has a heart, and gets his speeches by it.

HENRY LUTTRELL
1765?–1851

393   ON A MAN RUN OVER BY AN OMNIBUS

Killed by an omnibus—why not?
    So quick a death a boon is.
Let not his friends lament his lot—
    Mors omnibus communis.★

394   O death, thy certainty is such,
      And thou'rt a thing so fearful,
That, musing, I have wonder'd much
      How men were ever cheerful.

★ Death is common to all men.

ON A POET

Here lies a poet—where's the great surprise!
Since all men know, a poet deals in lies.
His patrons know, they don't deserve his praise:
He knows, he never meant it in his lays:
Knows, where he promises, he never pays.
Verse stands for sack, his knowledge for the score;
Both out, he's gone—where poets went before:
And at departing, let the waiters know
He'd pay his reck'ning in the realms below.

GEORGE CANNING
1770–1827

INSCRIPTION

*For the door of the cell in Newgate, where Mrs. Brownrigg, the
Prentice-cide, was confined previous to her Execution.*

For one long term, or e're her trial came,
Here BROWNRIGG linger'd. Often have these cells
Echoed her blasphemies, as with shrill voice
She scream'd for fresh Geneva. Not to her
Did the blithe fields of Tothill, or thy street,
St. Giles, its fair varieties expand;
Till at the last, in slow-drawn cart, she went
To execution. Dost thou ask her crime?
SHE WHIPP'D TWO FEMALE PRENTICES TO
  DEATH,
AND HID THEM IN THE COAL-HOLE. For her mind
Shaped strictest plans of discipline. Sage schemes!
Such as Lycurgus taught, when at the shrine
Of the Orthyan goddess he bade flog

The little Spartans; such as erst chastised
Our Milton, when at college. For this act
Did Brownrigg swing. Harsh laws! but time shall come,
When France shall reign, and laws be all repeal'd!

ANONYMOUS

397   ON RŸNEVELD, AN UNPOPULAR DUTCH
JUDGE AT THE CAPE OF GOOD HOPE

Here lies in death, who living always lied,
A base amalgam of deceit and pride;
A wily African of monstrous shape,
The mighty Quinbus Flestrin of the Cape.
Rogue paramount, ten thousand rogues among,
He rose and shone like phosphorus from dung;
The wolf and fox their attributes combined,
To form the odious features of his mind:
Where kennelled deep, by shame, by fear, unawed,
Lurk'd rapine, villainy, deceit, and fraud,
Hypocrisy, servility, and lust;
A petty tyrant, and a Judge unjust,
Partial and stern, in every cause he tried,
He judged like Pilate, and like Pilate died.
Urged to despair, by crimes precluding hope,
He chose a bullet, to avoid a rope.
Consistent knave! his life in cheating passed,
He shot himself, to cheat the law at last.
Acme of crimes, self-murder crowned the whole,
And gave to worms his corpse—to fiends his soul.

"Speak not of niceness, when there's chance of wreck," 398
The captain said, as ladies writhed their neck
To see the dying dolphin flap the deck:
"If we go down, on us these gentry sup;
We dine upon them, if we haul them up.
Wise men applaud us when we eat the eaters,
As the devil laughs when keen folks cheat the cheaters."

Sound, sound the clarion, fill the fife! 399
To all the sensual world proclaim,
One crowded hour of glorious life
Is worth an age without a name.

ON HAVING PILES 400

Ah dextrous Chirurgeons, mitigate your plan:
Slice bullock's rumps—but spare the rump of man.

TO-DAY I LEAVE
MRS. BROWN'S LODGINGS . . . 401

So good bye, Mrs. Brown,
I am going out of town
Over dale over down
Where bugs bite not
Where lodgers fight not
Where below you chairmen drink not
Where beside you gutters stink not
But all is fresh and clean and gay

And merry lambkins sport and play
And they toss with rakes uncommonly short hay
Which looks as if it had been sown only the other day
And where oats are at twenty five shillings a boll they say
But all's one for that since I must and will away.

SYDNEY SMITH?
1771–1845

402   BISHOP BLOMFIELD'S FIRST CHARGE
TO HIS CLERGY

Hunt not, fish not, shoot not,
Dance not, fiddle not, flute not;
Be sure ye have nothing to do with the Whigs,
But stay at home and feed your pigs;
And above all I make it my special desire,
That at least once a week you dine with the Squire.

403   ON SEEING FRANCIS JEFFREY
RIDING ON A DONKEY

Witty as Horatius Flaccus,
As great a Jacobin as Gracchus,
Short, though not as fat, as Bacchus,
Riding on a little jackass.

ANONYMOUS

404   ON DR. LETTSOM

If anybody comes to I,
I physics, bleeds, and sweats 'em;
If, after that, they like to die,
Why, what care I, I lets 'em.

Here lies the corpse of Doctor Chard,
Who fill'd half of this churchyard.

S. T. COLERIDGE
1772–1834

ON A BAD SINGER   406

Swans sing before they die: 't were no bad thing
Did certain persons die before they sing.

What is an Epigram? a dwarfish whole,   407
Its body brevity, and wit its soul.

Truth I pursued, as Fancy sketch'd the way,   408
And wiser men than I went worse astray.

EPITAPH ON HIMSELF   409

Here sleeps at length poor Col, and without screaming—
Who died as he had lived, a-dreaming:
Shot dead, while sleeping, by the gout within—
All alone and unknown, at Edinbro' in an inn.

MODERN CRITICS   410

No private grudge they need, no personal spite,
The *viva sectio* is its own delight!
All enmity, all envy, they disclaim,
Disinterested thieves of our good name:
Cool, sober murderers of their neighbours' fame.

W. H. *EHEU!*

Beneath this stone does William Hazlitt lie,
    Thankless of all that God or man could give.
He lived like one who never thought to die,
    He died like one who dared not hope to live.

412   COLOGNE

In Köln, a town of monks and bones,
And pavements fang'd with murderous stones,
And rags, and hags, and hideous wenches;
I counted two and seventy stenches,
All well defined, and several stinks!
Ye Nymphs that reign o'er sewers and sinks,
The river Rhine, it is well known,
Doth wash your city of Cologne;
But tell me, Nymphs! what power divine
Shall henceforth wash the river Rhine?

ANONYMOUS
413   CLONAKILTY

Galway is a blackguard place,
To Cork I give my curse,
Tralee itself is bad enough,
But Limerick is worse.
Which is worst I cannot tell,
They're everyone so filthy,
But of the towns which I have seen
Worst luck to Clonakilty.

ON PETER ROBINSON   414

Here lies the preacher, judge, and poet, Peter
Who broke the laws of God, and man, and metre.

WALTER SAVAGE LANDOR
1775–1864

EPIGRAMS   415

Epigrams must be curt, nor seem
Tail-pieces to a poet's dream.
If they should anywhere be found
Serious, or musical in sound
Turn into prose the two worst pages
And you will rank among the sages.

ON A QUAKER'S TANKARD   416

Ye lie, friend Pindar! and friend Thales!—
Nothing so good as water? Ale is.

Poet! I like not mealy fruit; give me   417
Freshness and crispness and solidity;
Apples are none the better overripe,
And prime buck-venison I prefer to tripe.

TO POETS

Patience! coy singers of the Delphic wood,
The brightest sun tempts forth the viper brood;
And, of all insects buds and blooms enclose,
The one that stinks the most infests the rose.

419   A CRITIC

With much ado you fail to tell
The requisites for writing well;
But what bad writing is, you quite
Have proved by every line you write.

420   Why do the Graces now desert the Muse?
They hate bright ribbons tying wooden shoes.

421   TO ONE WHO QUOTES AND DETRACTS

Rob me and maim me! Why, man, take such pains
On your bare heath to hang yourself in chains?

422   Why should scribblers discompose
Our temper? would we look like those?
There are some curs in every street
Who snarl and snap at all they meet:
The taller mastiff deems it aptest
To lift a leg and play the baptist.

Ten thousand flakes about my windows blow,
Some falling and some rising, but all snow.
Scribblers and statesmen! are ye not just so?

423

Ireland never was contented.
Say you so? You are demented.
Ireland was contented when
All could use the sword and pen,
And when Tara rose so high
That her turrets split the sky,
And about her courts were seen
Liveried angels robed in green,
Wearing, by St. Patrick's bounty,
Emeralds big as half the county.

424

THE GEORGES

425

George the First was always reckoned
Vile, but viler George the Second;
And what mortal ever heard
Any good of George the Third?
When from earth the Fourth descended
(God be praised!) the Georges ended.

Enduring is the bust of bronze,
And thine, O flower of George's sons,
Stands high above all laws and duns.

As honest men as ever cart
Convey'd to Tyburn took thy part
And raised thee up to where thou art.

427   A QUARRELSOME BISHOP

To hide her ordure, claws the cat;
You claw, but not to cover that.
Be decenter, and learn at least
One lesson from the cleanlier beast.

428   Clap, clap the double nightcap on!
        Gifford will read you his amours . . .
    Lazy as Scheld and cold as Don.
        Kneel, and thank Heaven they are not yours.

429   Exhausted now her sighs, and dry her tears,
    For twenty youths these more than twenty years,
    Anne, turning nun, swears God alone shall have her.
    God ought to bow profoundly for the favour.

"OUR COUCH SHALL BE ROSES ALL SPANGLED WITH DEW"
It would give me rheumatics, and so it would you.

DISTRIBUTION OF HONOURS   431
FOR LITERATURE

The grandest writer of late ages
Who wrapt Rome up in golden pages,
Whom scarcely Livius equal'd, Gibbon,
Died without star or cross or ribbon.

Had we two met, blythe-hearted Burns,   432
   Tho water is my daily drink,
   May God forgive me but I think
We should have roared out toasts by turns.

Inquisitive low-whispering cares
   Had found no room in either pate,
   Until I asked thee, rather late,
Is there a hand-rail to the stairs?

Neither in idleness consume thy days,   433
Nor bend thy back to mow the weeds of praise.

There are two miseries in human life;   434
To live without a friend, and with a wife.

435

Triumphant Demons stand, and Angels start,
To see the abysses of the human heart.

436   REFLECTION FROM SEA AND SKY

When I gaze upon the sky
And the sea below, I cry,
Thus be poetry and love,
Deep beneath and bright above.

437   God scatters beauty as he scatters flowers
O'er the wide earth, and tells us all are ours.
A hundred lights in every temple burn,
And at each shrine I bend my knee in turn.

438   DIRCE

Stand close around, ye Stygian set,
    With Dirce in one boat conveyed!
Or Charon, seeing, may forget
    That he is old and she a shade.

439   How often, when life's summer day
    Is waning, and its sun descends,
Wisdom drives laughing wit away,
    And lovers shrivel into friends!

Lately our poets loiter'd in green lanes, 440
Content to catch the ballads of the plains;
I fancied I had strength to climb
A loftier station at no distant time,
And might securely from intrusion doze
Upon the flowers thro' which Ilissus flows.
In those pale olive grounds all voices cease,
And from afar dust fills the paths of Greece.
My slumber broken and my doublet torn,
I find the laurel also bears a thorn.

ON THE HEIGHTS 441

The cattle in the common field
    Toss their flat heads in vain,
And snort and stamp; weak creatures yield
    And turn back home again.

My mansion stands beyond it, high
    Above where rushes grow;
Its hedge of laurel dares defy
    The heavy-hooft below.

The scentless laurel a broad leaf displays, 442
Few and by fewer gather'd are the bays;
Yet these Apollo wore upon his brow.
The boughs are bare, the stem is twisted now.

443   Our youth was happy: why repine
       That, like the Year's, Life's days decline?
       'Tis well to mingle with the mould
       When we ourselves alike are cold,
       And when the only tears we shed
       Are of the dying on the dead.

444   Various the roads of life; in one
           All terminate, one lonely way.
       We go; and "Is he gone?"
           Is all our best friends say.

445   FOR AN EPITAPH AT FIESOLE

       Lo! where the four mimosas blend their shade,
       In calm repose at last is Landor laid;
       For ere he slept he saw them planted here
       By her his soul had ever held most dear,
       And he had lived enough when he had dried her tear.

446   ON HIMSELF

       Come forth, old lion, from thy den,
       Come, be the gaze of idle men,
       Old lion, shake thy mane and growl,
       Or they will take thee for an owl.

I strove with none, for none was worth my strife:
    Nature I loved, and, next to Nature, Art:
I warm'd both hands before the fire of Life;
    It sinks; and I am ready to depart.

AGE   448

Death, tho I see him not, is near
And grudges me my eightieth year.
Now, I would give him all these last
For one that fifty have run past.
Ah! he strikes all things, all alike,
But bargains: those he will not strike.

No charm can stay, no medicine can assuage,   449
The sad incurable disease of age;
Only the hand in youth more warmly prest
Makes soft the couch and calms the final rest.

Above all gifts we most should prize   450
The wisdom that makes others wise;
To others when ourselves are dust
We leave behind this sacred trust,
We may not know, when we are gone,
The good we shall on earth have done;
Enough in going is the thought
For once we acted as we ought.

451   Here lies Landor,
              Whom they thought a goose,
              But he proved a gander.

THOMAS MOORE
1779–1852

452   NONSENSE

        Good reader! if you e'er have seen,
            When Phoebus hastens to his pillow,
        The mermaids, with their tresses green,
            Dancing upon the western billow:
        If you have seen, at twilight dim,
        When the long spirit's vesper hymn
            Floats wild along the western shore,
        If you have seen, through mist of eve,
        The fairy train their ringlets weave,
        Glancing along the spangled green:—
            If you have seen all this, and more,
        God bless me, what a deal you've seen!

453   EPITAPH ON A TUFT-HUNTER

        Lament, lament, Sir Isaac Heard,
            Put mourning round thy page, Debrett,
        For here lies one, who ne'er preferr'd
            A Viscount to a Marquis yet.

        Beside him place the God of Wit,
            Before him Beauty's rosiest girls,
        Apollo for a *star* he'd quit,
            And Love's own sister for an Earl's.

Did niggard fate no peers afford,
    He took, of course, to peers' relations;
And, rather than not sport a Lord,
    Put up with even the last creations.

Even Irish names, could he but tag 'em
    With "Lord" and "Duke", were sweet to call;
And, at a pinch, Lord Ballyraggum
    Was better than no Lord at all.

Heaven grant him now some noble nook,
    For, rest his soul! he'd rather be
Genteelly damn'd beside a Duke,
    Than sav'd in vulgar company.

WHAT'S MY THOUGHT LIKE?   454

Quest. Why is a Pump like Viscount Castlereagh?
Answ. Because it is a slender thing of wood
    That up and down its awkward arm doth sway,
    And coolly spout and spout and spout away,
In one weak, washy, everlasting flood!

IRISH ANTIQUITIES   455

According to some learn'd opinions
The Irish once were Carthaginians;
But, trusting to more late descriptions,
I'd rather say they were Egyptians.
My reason's this:- the Priests of Isis,
    When forth they march'd in long array,
Employ'd, 'mong other grave devices,
    A Sacred Ass to lead the way;

And still the antiquarian traces
'Mong Irish lords this pagan plan,
For still, in all religious cases,
They put Lord Roden in the van.

EPITAPH ON ROBERT SOUTHEY

Beneath these poppies buried deep,
The bones of Bob the bard lie hid;
Peace to his manes; and may he sleep
As soundly as his readers did!

Through every sort of verse meandering,
Bob went without a hitch or fall,
Through epic, Sapphic, Alexandrine,
To verse that was no verse at all;

Till fiction having done enough,
To make a bard at least absurd,
And give his readers *quantum suff.*,
He took to praising George the Third,

And now, in virtue of his crown,
Dooms us, poor whigs, at once to slaughter;
Like Donellan of bad renown,
Poisoning us all with laurel water.

And yet at times some awful qualms he
Felt about leaving honour's track;
And though he's got a butt of Malmsey,
It may not save him from a sack.

Death, weary of so dull a writer,
Put to his books a *finis* thus.
Oh! may the earth on him lie lighter
Than did his quartos upon us!

Reader, pass on, nor idly waste your time,　　457
In bad biography, or bitter rhyme;
What I am, this cumbrous clay ensures,
And what I was is no affair of yours.

(after the Greek of Paulos)★

ON QUEEN CAROLINE　　458

Most Gracious Queen, we thee implore
To go away and sin no more,
But if that effort be too great,
To go away at any rate.

ON TOM ONSLOW, EARL OF ONSLOW　　459

What can little T.O. do?
　　Why, drive a phaeton and two.
Can little T.O. do no more?
　　Why, drive a phaeton and four.

★ For Cowper's version see No. 342.

Here lies Fred
Who was alive and is dead:
Had it been his father,
I had much rather;
Had it been his brother,
Still better than another;
Had it been his sister,
No one would have missed her;
Had it been the whole generation,
So much the better for the nation;
But since 'tis only Fred
Who was alive and is dead,—
Why, there's no more to be said.

461

When you look on my grave,
    And behold how they wave,
The cypress, the yew, and the willow,
    You think 'tis the breeze,
    That gives motion to these—
'Tis the laughter that's shaking my pillow.
    I must laugh when I see
    A poor insect like thee
Dare to pity the fate thou must own,
    Let a few moments slide,
    We shall lie side by side,
And crumble to dust bone for bone.
    Go, weep thine own doom,
    Thou wert born for the tomb—
Thou hast lived, like myself, but to die.
    Whilst thou pity'st my lot,
    Secure fool, thou'st forgot
Thou art no more immortal than I.

WHAT JENNER SAID ON HEARING IN   462
ELYSIUM THAT COMPLAINTS HAD BEEN MADE
OF HIS HAVING A STATUE IN TRAFALGAR SQUARE

England's ingratitude still blots
The scutcheon of the brave and free;
I saved you from a million spots,
And now you grudge a spot to me.

EBENEZER ELLIOTT
1781–1849

ON A ROSE IN DECEMBER   463

Stay yet, pale flower, though coming storms will tear thee,
My soul grows darker, and I cannot spare thee.

BEWARE OF DOGMAS   464

Two pilgrims, broiling in the sun,
Did once to Glasgow come.
Each had but twopence. James bought rum,
With all his cash; and Charles a bun—
Of his two pennies saving one.
Charles died of fever in a week!
James lives and thrives, is stout and sleek,
And keeps, abjuring rum and gin,
A Temperance inn.

Here lies the man who stripp'd Sin bare,
And kept her lean, on hard-earn'd fare;
Who forc'd the poor at home to stay,
But rode to church on Sabbath day;
And went to heav'n, the sinless say,
Because he bother'd God with prayer,
And would not let him have his way.

466 EPIGRAM

Paddy, I have but stol'n your living
    And call'd you names beside:
Why are not you content and thankful,
    If I am satisfied?
As I have done, so did my father,
    And full of peace he died.

GEORGE GORDON, LORD BYRON
1788–1824

467 EPITAPH FOR WILLIAM PITT

With death doom'd to grapple,
    Beneath this cold slab, he
Who lied in the Chapel
    Now lies in the Abbey.

Who kill'd John Keats?
  "I," says the Quarterly,
So savage and Tartarly;
  "'Twas one of my feats."

Who shot the arrow?
  "The poet-priest Milman
(So ready to kill man)
  Or Southey, or Barrow."

EPITAPH   469

Posterity will ne'er survey
  A nobler grave than this:
Here lie the bones of Castlereagh:
  Stop, traveller, and piss.

STANZAS   470

When a man hath no freedom to fight for at home,
  Let him combat for that of his neighbours;
Let him think of the glories of Greece and of Rome,
  And get knock'd on the head for his labours.

To do good to mankind is the chivalrous plan,
  And is always as nobly requited;
Then battle for freedom wherever you can,
  And, if not shot or hang'd, you'll get knighted.

> He unto whom thou art so partial,
> Oh, reader! is the well-known Martial,
> The Epigrammatist: while living,
> Give him the fame thou wouldst be giving;
> So shall he hear, and feel, and know it—
>   Post obits rarely reach a poet.

472

> This day of all our days has done
>   The worst for me and you;
> 'Tis now six years since we were *one*,
>   And five since we were *two*.

473
ON MY THIRTY-THIRD BIRTHDAY
JANUARY 22, 1821

> Through life's dull road, so dim and dirty,
> I have dragg'd to three-and-thirty.
> What have these years left to me?
> Nothing—except thirty-three.

R. H. BARHAM
1788–1845
474   *EHEU FUGACES*

> What Horace says is—
> *Eheu fugaces*
> *Anni labuntur, Postume, Postume!*
> Years glide away, and are lost to me, lost to me!
> *Now*, when folks in the dance sport their merry toes,
> Taglionis and Ellslers, Duvernays and Ceritos,
> Sighing I murmur, *O mihi praeteritos!*

CHARLES TOWNSEND
1789–1870

ON THE LAKE POETS   475

They live by the Lakes, an appropriate quarter
For poems diluted with plenty of water.

P. B. SHELLEY
1792–1822

ON KEATS   476
WHO DESIRED THAT ON HIS TOMB
SHOULD BE INSCRIBED—

"Here lieth one whose name was writ on water."
  But, ere the breath that could erase it blew,
Death, in remorse for that fell slaughter,
  Death, the immortalizing winter, flew
  Athwart the stream,—and time's printless torrent grew
A scroll of crystal, blazoning the name
  Of Adonais!

TO STELLA   477

Thou wert the morning star among the living
  Ere thy fair light had fled;—
Now, having died, thou art as Hesperus, giving
  New splendour to the dead.

(After the Greek of Plato)

JOHN CLARE
1793–1864

478   Language has not the power to speak what love indites:
        The Soul lies buried in the ink that writes.

ANONYMOUS

479   INQUESTS EXTRAORDINARY

                              I

                ON THE MEANNESS OF LORD ELDON
        Found dead a rat—no case could sure be harder;
        Verdict—Confined a week in Eldon's larder.

                              II

                ON THE UNCLEANLY HABITS OF
                    SIR CHARLES WETHERELL
        Died from fatigue, three laundresses together all;
        Verdict—Had tried to wash a shirt marked Wetherell.

                              III

                        ON THE SAME
        Died, Sir Charles Wetherell's laundress, honest Sue;
        Verdict—Ennui, so little work to do.

480   TO THE ARCHBISHOP OF TUAM

                        Had everyone Suum,
                        You wouldn't have Tuum,
                        But I should have Meum
                        And sing Te Deum.

In ancient times—'twas no great loss—
They hung the thief upon the cross:
But now, alas!—I say't with grief—
They hang the cross upon the thief.

(From the French)

THOMAS HOOD
1799–1845

A REFLECTION   482

When Eve upon the first of Men
    The apple press'd with specious cant
Oh! what a thousand pities then
    That Adam was not adamant!

DEDICATION, TO THE REVIEWERS   483

What is a modern Poet's fate?
To write his thoughts upon a slate;—
The Critic spits on what is done,—
Gives it a wipe,—and all is gone.

⟨ON THE PUBLICATION OF DIARIES   484
AND MEMOIRS⟩

The poor dear dead have been laid out in vain,
Turn'd into cash, they are laid out again!

They say, God wot!
She died upon the spot:
But then in spots she was so rich,—
I wonder which?

ANONYMOUS
486   ON AN ABERDEEN FAVOURITE

Here lie the bones of Elizabeth Charlotte,
That was born a virgin and died a harlot.
She was aye a virgin till seventeen—
An extraordinary thing for Aberdeen.

487   ON THE REVEREND JONATHAN DOE

Here lies the Reverend Jonathan Doe,
Where he has gone to I don't know:
If haply to the realms above,
Farewell to happiness and love,
If haply to a lower level,
I can't congratulate the Devil.

Here lies the body of William Jones
Who all his life collected bones,
Till Death, that grim and boney spectre,
That universal bone collector,
Boned old Jones, so neat and tidy,
And here he lies, all *bona fide*.

THOMAS LOVELL BEDDOES
1803–1849

RESURRECTION SONG 489

Thread the nerves through the right holes,
Get out of my bones, you wormy souls.
Shut up my stomach, the ribs are full:
Muscles be steady and ready to pull.
Heart and artery merrily shake
And eyelid go up, for we're ready to wake.—
His eye must be brighter—one more rub!
And pull up the nostrils! his nose was snub.

BENJAMIN HALL KENNEDY
1804–1889

ON A BOOK ENTITLED "WHO WROTE ICON 490
BASILIKE", BY DR. CHRISTOPHER
WORDSWORTH, MASTER OF TRINITY
COLLEGE, CAMBRIDGE

Who wrote "Who wrote Icon Basilike?"
I, said the Master of Trinity,
With my small ability
I wrote "Who wrote Icon Basilike".

OLD FORTY-FIVE PER CENT

Here lies old Forty-Five Per Cent;
The more he got the more he lent,
The more he saved, the more he craved:
Great God! can such a soul be saved?

492

Here lies Sir John Plumpudding of the Grange,
Who hanged himself one morning for a change.

493

Two sweeter babes you nare did see
Than God A'mighty gave to we,
But they wer ortaken wi ague fits
And here they lies as dead as nits.

494

Here lies a poor woman who always was tired,
She lived in a house where no help wasn't hired.
The last words she said were "Dear friends, I am going,
Where washing an't wanted, nor mending, nor sewing.
There all things is done just exact to my wishes,
For where folk don't eat there's no washing of dishes.
In Heaven loud anthems for ever are ringing,
But having no voice, I'll keep clear of the singing.
Don't mourn for me now, don't mourn for me never;
I'm going to do nothing for ever and ever."

They built the front, upon my word,
  As fine as any abbey;
But thinking they might cheat the Lord,
  They made the back part shabby.

ON THE DEATH OF THE GREAT CHEF   496
ALEXIS SOYER

Soyer is gone! Then be it said,
Indeed, indeed, great Pan is dead.

ALFRED, LORD TENNYSON
1809–1892

In my youth the growls!   497
In mine age the owls!
After death the ghouls!

TO CHRISTOPHER NORTH   498

You did late review my lays,
  Crusty Christopher;
You did mingle blame and praise,
  Rusty Christopher.
When I learnt from whom it came,
I forgave you all the blame,
  Musty Christopher;
I could not forgive the praise,
  Fusty Christopher.

499   Somebody being a nobody,
                Thinking to look like a somebody,
                Said he thought me a nobody:
                Good little somebody-nobody,
                Had you not known me a somebody,
                Would you have called me a nobody?

500   I ran upon life unknowing, without or science or art,
       I found the first pretty maiden but she was a harlot at heart;
       I wandered about the woodland after the melting of snow,
       "Here is the first pretty snowdrop"—and it was the dung of a
          crow!

501   ⟨ON SUPPORTERS OF THE
              BACONIAN THEORY⟩

              Not only with no sense of shame
              On common-sense you tread,
              Not only ride your hobby lame,
              But make him kick the dead.

502   ⟨ON HIS PUBLISHER⟩

              Ancient Pistol, peacock Payne,
              Brute in manner, rogue in grain,
              How you squeezed me, peacock Payne!
              Scared was I and out I ran
              And found by Paul's an honest man.
              Peace be with you, peacock Payne,
              I have left you, you remain
              Ancient Pistol, sealskin Payne.

Immeasurable sadness!
And I know it as a poet,
And I greet it, and I meet it,
Immeasurable sadness!
And the voice that apes a nation—
Let it cry "An affectation,"
Or "A fancy" or "A madness,"—
But I know it as a poet,
And I meet it, and I greet it,
And I say it, and repeat it,
Immeasurable sadness!

W. M. THACKERAY
1811–1863

THE GEORGES 504

GEORGE I,—STAR OF BRUNSWICK

He preferr'd Hanover to England,
He preferr'd two hideous mistresses
To a beautiful and innocent wife.
He hated arts and despised literature;
But he liked train-oil in his salads,
And gave an enlighten'd patronage to bad oysters.
And he had Walpole as a minister;
Consistent in his preference for every kind of corruption.

GEORGE II

In most things I did as my father had done,
I was false to my wife and I hated my son:
My spending was small, and my avarice much,
My kingdom was English, my heart was High-Dutch:

At Dettingen fight I was not known to blench,
I butcher'd the Scotch, and I bearded the French:
I neither had morals, nor manners, nor wit;
I wasn't much miss'd when I died in a fit.
Here set up my statue, and make it complete,
With Pitt on his knees at my dirty old feet.

GEORGE III

Give me a royal niche—it is my due,
The virtuousest king the realm ever knew.
I through a decent reputable life
Was constant to plain food, and a plain wife.
Ireland I risk'd, and lost America;
But dined on legs of mutton every day.
My brain, perhaps, might be a feeble part;
Yet I think I had an English heart:
When all kings were prostrate, I alone
Stood face to face against Napoleon.
Nor ever could the ruthless Frenchman forge
A fetter for Old England and Old George.
I let loose flaming Nelson on his fleets;
I met his troops with Wellesley's bayonets.
Triumphant waved my flag on land and sea;
Where was the king in Europe like to me?
Monarchs exiled found shelter on my shores,
My bounty rescued kings and emperors.
But what boots victory by land or sea?
What boots that kings found refuge at my knee?
I was a conqueror, but yet not proud;
And careless, even though Napoleon bow'd.
The rescued kings came kiss my garment's hem,
The rescued kings I never heeded them.
My guns roar'd triumph ,but I never heard;
All England thrill'd with joy, I never stirr'd.

What care had I of pomp, of fame, or power,
A crazy old blind man in Windsor Tower?

GEORGE IV

He never acted well by man or woman,
And was as false to his mistress as to his wife.
He deserted his friends and his principles.
He was so ignorant that he could scarcely spell;
But he had some skill in cutting out coats,
And an undeniable taste for cookery.
He built the palaces of Brighton and of Buckingham,
And for these qualities and proofs of genius,
An admiring aristocracy
Christen'd him the "First Gentleman in Europe."
Friends, respect the king whose statue is here,
And the generous aristocracy who admired him.

H. J. DANIEL
1818–1889

MY EPITAPH   505

Here lies a bard, let epitaphs be true,
His vices many, and his virtues few;
Who always left religion in the lurch
But never left a tavern for a church,
Drank more from pewter than Pierian spring
And only in his cups was known to sing;
Laugh'd at the world, however it may blame,
And died regardless of his fate or fame.

HERMAN MELVILLE
1819–1891

506   THE TUFT OF KELP

All dripping in tangles green,
    Cast up by a lonely sea,
If purer for that, O Weed,
    Bitterer, too, are ye?

ARTHUR HUGH CLOUGH
1819–1861

507   THE LATEST DECALOGUE

Thou shalt have one God only, who
Would be at the expense of two?
No graven images may be
Worshipped, except the currency:
Swear not at all, for for thy curse
Thine enemy is none the worse:
At church on Sunday to attend
Will serve to keep the world thy friend:
Honour thy parents; that is, all
From whom advancement may befall:
Thou shalt not kill; but needst not strive
Officiously to keep alive:
Do not adultery commit;
Advantage rarely comes of it:
Thou shalt not steal; an empty feat,
When it's so lucrative to cheat:
Bear not false witness; let the lie
Have time on its own wings to fly:
Thou shalt not covet; but tradition
Approves all forms of competition.

The sum of all is, thou shalt love,
If any body, God above:
At any rate shall never labour
More than thyself to love thy neighbour.

A. C. SWINBURNE
1837–1909

ON ARTHUR HUGH CLOUGH   508

There was a bad poet named Clough
Whom his friends found it useless to puff;
    For the public, if dull,
    Has not quite such a skull
As belongs to believers in Clough.

MATTHEW ARNOLD
1822–1888

A NAMELESS EPITAPH   509

This sentence have I left behind:
An aching body, and a mind
Not wholly clear, nor wholly blind,
Too keen to rest, too weak to find,
That travails sore, and brings forth wind,
Are God's worst portion to mankind.

ANONYMOUS
Here lies my dear wife, a sad slattern and a shrew.   510
If I said I regretted her, I should lie too.

511   Here lies I and my three daughters,
Killed by drinking the Cheltenham waters.
If we had stuck to our Epsom salts
We'd not be lying in these vaults.

512   Beneath this stone, in hope of Zion,
Doth lie the landlord of the "Lion".
His son keeps on the business still,
Resign'd unto the Heavenly will.

513   EPITAPH

Here lies a man who was killed by lightning;
He died when his prospects seemed to be brightening.
He might have cut a flash in this world of trouble,
But the flash cut him, and he lies in the stubble.

514   ON ELIZABETH IRELAND

Here I lie at the chancel door,
Here I lie because I'm poor:
The further in, the more you pay:
Here lie I as warm as they.

515   TAMMY MESSER

Here lie the banes o' Tammy Messer,
O' tarry woo' he was a dresser,
He had some faults and many merits,
And died of drinking ardent spirits.

ON WILLIAM WILSON, TAILOR

Here lies the body of W. W.,
Who never more will trouble you, trouble you.

EPITAPH ON AN IRISH PRIEST

Here I lie for the last time,
Lying has been my pastime,
And now I've joined the Heavenly choir
I hope I still may play the lyre.

COVENTRY PATMORE
1823–1896

THE ATTAINMENT 518

You love? That's high as you shall go;
    For 'tis as true as Gospel text,
Not noble then is never so,
    Either in this world or the next.

PERSPECTIVE 519

What seems to us for us is true.
    The planet has no proper light,
And yet, when Venus is in view,
    No primal star is half so bright.

A bee upon a briar-rose hung
And wild with pleasure suck'd and kiss'd;
A flesh-fly near, with snout in dung,
Sneer'd, "What a Transcendentalist!"

521 ⟨PAIN IN ALL LOVE⟩

From the small life that loves with tooth and nail
To the thorn'd brow that makes the heavens pale.

522 How fair a flower is sown
When Knowledge goes, with fearful tread,
To the dark bed
Of the divine Unknown!

523 Science, the agile ape, may well
Up in his tree thus grin and grind his teeth
At us beneath,
The wearers of the bay and asphodel,
Laughing to be his butts,
And gathering up for use his ill-aim'd cocoa-nuts.

524 Save by the Old Road none attain the new,
And from the Ancient Hills alone we catch the view.

⟨KING WILLIAM'S DISPATCH TO QUEEN   525
AUGUSTA, AFTER THE BATTLE OF WOERTH
IN THE FRANCO-PRUSSIAN WAR⟩

This is to say, my dear Augusta,
We've had another awful buster,
Ten thousand Frenchmen sent below!
Thank God from whom all blessings flow!

ANONYMOUS

THE FRENCH, 1870–1871   526

The Cock of Glory is the *coq français*,
  Who's never silent when he's beat.
Loud as he crows when he has won the day,
  He crows more loudly in defeat.

WILLIAM ALLINGHAM
1824–1889

A MILL   527

Two leaps the water from its race
  Made to the brook below,
The first leap it was curving glass,
  The second bounding snow.

528   A SUGGESTION MADE BY THE POSTERS OF
THE "GLOBE"

The Globe, a paper of the Tories
(See the big posters stuck up here),
Depicts the name in which it glories,
And maps the southern hemisphere.

And oddly, too, it takes the pains
To symbolise its readers' worth,
For that same hemisphere contains
The lowest savages on earth.

529   ON A DISTINGUISHED POLITICIAN

Greatest in many things, in some the least,
He reverenced what the wise have all abhorred,
Was more than half a mystic with a priest,
And more than half a lackey to a lord.

530   AN EPITAPH

Here X. lies dead, but God's forgiving,
And shows compassion to the living.

531   ANOTHER

Upon the man who's buried here
Drop anything except a tear.

Pleasure and pride are not, as duty knows,
(Though parsons think them) virtue's deadliest foes;
The vice which always serves the Devil best
(Perhaps the parson) is self-interest.

ON THE HISTORIANS FREEMAN AND STUBBS   533

While ladling butter from alternate tubs,
Stubbs butters Freeman, Freeman butters Stubbs.

WILLIAM STUBBS
1825–1901

A HYMN ON FROUDE AND KINGSLEY   534

Froude informs the Scottish youth
That parsons do not care for truth.
The Reverend Canon Kingsley cries
History is a pack of lies.
What cause for judgments so malign?
    A brief reflexion solves the mystery—
Froude believes Kingsley a divine,
    And Kingsley goes to Froude for history.

ANONYMOUS

535 OF THE PRINCIPAL AND VICE-PRINCIPAL OF THE LADIES' COLLEGE, CHELTENHAM

Miss Buss and Miss Beale
Cupid's darts do not feel.
How different from us,
Miss Beale and Miss Buss.

536 FROM THE *BALLIOL RHYMES*, WRITTEN IN 1881

I

ON BENJAMIN JOWETT, MASTER OF BALLIOL

First come I. My name is Jowett.
There's no knowledge but I know it.
I am Master of this College,
What I don't know isn't knowledge.

H. C. Beeching

II

ON JOHN WILLIAM MACKAIL, FELLOW OF BALLIOL

I am rather tall and stately
And I care not very greatly
What you say or what you do:
I'm Mackail—and who are you?

Anon

III

ON SOLOMON LAZARUS LEE, EXHIBITIONER OF BALLIOL

I am featly-tripping Lee,
Learned in modern history,
My gown, the wonder of beholders
Hangs like a foot-note from my shoulders.

H. C. Beeching

IV

ON THE HON. GEORGE NATHANIEL CURZON, COMMONER OF BALLIOL

My name is George Nathaniel Curzon,
I am a most superior person.
My cheeks are pink, my hair is sleek,
I dine at Blenheim twice a week.

J. W. Mackail and Cecil Spring-Rice

V

ON CLINTON EDWARD DAWKINS, COMMONER OF BALLIOL

Positivists ever talk in s-
Uch an epic style as Dawkins;
Creeds are naught and Man is all,
Spell Him with a capital.

J. W. Mackail

VI

ON J. C. E. BRANSON,
COMMONER OF BALLIOL

I am Branson; Nature's laws
Govern all things; some first cause
May exist, but I don't know;
It's Nature makes my whiskers grow.

H. C. Beeching and J. B. Nichols

VII

ON SIR WILLIAM ANSON,
FELLOW OF ALL SOULS

I'm the great Sir William Anson,
Versed alike in Coke and Hanson.
All Souls claret is a boon:
I belong to All Souls—soon
If the fates and I agree
All Souls will belong to me.

Anon

VIII

ON HENRY GEORGE LIDDELL
DEAN OF CHRIST CHURCH

I am the Dean of Christ Church, Sir,
This is my wife—look well at her.
She is the Broad: I am the High:
We are the University.

Cecil Spring-Rice

IX

ANOTHER VERSION OF THE LINES ON
THE DEAN OF CHRIST CHURCH

I am the Dean, and this is Mrs. Liddell:
She plays the first, and I the second fiddle.
She is the Broad: I am the High:
We are the University.

DANTE GABRIEL ROSSETTI
1828–1882

ON THE PAINTER VAL PRINSEP   537

There is a creator named God
Whose creations are some of them odd.
I maintain, and I shall, the creation of Val
Reflects little credit on God.

ON THE SAME   538

There is a big artist named Val,
The roughs' and the prizefighters' pal:
The mind of a groom, and the head of a broom,
Were nature's endowments to Val.

ON WHISTLER   539

There's a combative artist named Whistler
Who is, like his own hog's-hairs, a bristler:
A tube of white lead and a punch on the head
Offer varied attractions to Whistler.

There are dealers in pictures named Agnew
Whose soft soap would make an old rag new:
The Father of Lies, with his tail to his eyes,
Cries—"Go to it, Tom Agnew, Bill Agnew!"

541   ON GAMBART THE ART DEALER

There is an old he-wolf named Gambart;
Beware of him if thou a lamb art,
Else thy tail and thy toes and thine innocent nose
Will be ground by the grinders of Gambart.

542   ON ROBERT BUCHANAN, WHO ATTACKED HIM UNDER THE PSEUDONYM OF "THOMAS MAITLAND."

As a critic the poet Buchanan
Thinks "Pseudo" much safer than "Anon."
Into Maitland he's shrunk, yet the smell of the skunk
Guides the shuddering nose to Buchanan.

543   ON HIMSELF

There is a poor sneak called Rossetti;
As a painter with many kicks met he—
With more as a man—but sometimes he ran,
And that saved the rear of Rossetti.

Lad of Athens, faithful be   544
To Thyself,
And Mystery—
All the rest is Perjury.

Ourselves we do inter with sweet derision,   545
The charnel of the dust who once achieves
Invalidates the balm of that religion
That doubts as fervently as it believes.

To flee from memory   546
Had we the Wings
Many would fly
Inured to slower things
Birds with surprise
Would scan the cowering Van
Of men escaping
From the mind of man.

There is no Silence in the Earth—so silent   547
As that endured
Which uttered, would discourage Nature
And haunt the World.

CHRISTINA ROSSETTI
1830–1894

548   What are heavy? sea-sand and sorrow:
                    What are brief? to-day and to-morrow:
                    What are frail? Spring blossoms and youth:
                    What are deep? the ocean and truth.

549   I dug and dug amongst the snow,
                    And thought the flowers would never grow;
                    I dug and dug amongst the sand,
                    And still no green thing came to hand.

                    Melt, O snow! the warm winds blow
                    To thaw the flowers and melt the snow;
                    But all the winds from every land
                    Will rear no blossom from the sand.

C. S. CALVERLEY
1831–1884

550   EPITAPH OF CLEONICUS

           Man, husband existence: ne'er launch on the sea
              Out of season: our tenure of life is but frail.
        Think of poor Cleonicus: for Phasos sailed he
              From the valleys of Syria, with many a bale:
        With many a bale, ocean's tides he would stem
        When the Pleiads were sinking; and he sank with them.

                                  (After the Greek of Theokritos)

Friend, Ortho of Syracuse gives thee this charge:
    Never venture out, drunk, on a wild winter's night.
I did so and died. My possessions were large;
    Yet the turf that I'm clad with is strange to me quite.

(After the Greek of Theokritos)

EPITAPH OF HIPPONAX   552

Tuneful Hipponax rests him here.
Let no base rascal venture near.
You who rank high in birth and mind
Sit down—and sleep, if so inclined.

(After the Greek of Theokritos)

WILLIAM CORY
1832–1892

HERACLITUS   553

They told me, Heraclitus, they told me you were dead,
They brought me bitter news to hear and bitter tears to shed.
I wept as I remember'd how often you and I
Had tired the sun with talking and sent him down the sky.

And now that thou art lying, my dear old Carian guest,
A handful of grey ashes, long, long ago at rest,
Still are thy pleasant voices, thy *Nightingales*, awake;
For Death, he taketh all away, but them he cannot take.

(After the Greek of Kallimachos)

LEWIS CARROLL
1832–1896

554   HOW DOTH...

How doth the little crocodile
    Improve his shining tail,
And pour the waters of the Nile
    On every golden scale!

How cheerfully he seems to grin,
    How neatly spreads his claws,
And welcomes little fishes in
    With gently smiling jaws!

SAMUEL BUTLER THE SECOND
1835–1902

555   A PRAYER

Searcher of souls, you who in heaven abide,
To whom the secrets of all hearts are open,
Though I do lie to all the world beside,
From me to thee no falsehood shall be spoken.
Cleanse me not, Lord, I say, from secret sin
But from those faults which he who runs can see.
'Tis these that torture me, O Lord, begin
With these and let the hidden vices be;
If you must cleanse these too, at any rate
Deal with the seen sins first, 'tis only reason,
They being so gross, to let the others wait
The leisure of some more convenient season;
    And cleanse not all even then, leave me a few,
    I would not be—not quite—so pure as you.

THE PIG

It was an evening in November,
As I very well remember,
I was strolling down the street in drunken pride,
But my knees were all a-flutter,
And I landed in the gutter
And a pig came up and lay down by my side.

Yes, I lay there in the gutter
Thinking thoughts I could not utter,
When a colleen passing by did softly say
"Ye can tell a man that boozes
By the company he chooses."—
And the pig got up and walked away.

JOHN MILTON HAY
1838–1905

DISTICH 557

What is a first love worth except to prepare for a second?
What does the second love bring? Only regret for the first.

Good Luck is the gayest of all gay girls;
    Long in one place she will not stay:
Back from your brow she strokes the curls,
    Kisses you quick and flies away.

But Madame Bad Luck soberly comes
    And stays—no fancy has she for flitting,—
Snatches of true-love songs she hums,
    And sits by your bed, and brings her knitting.

(After the German of Heine)

THOMAS HARDY
1840–1928

559   A NECESSITARIAN'S EPITAPH

A world I did not wish to enter
Took me and poised me on my centre,
Made me grimace, and foot, and prance,
As cats on hot bricks have to dance
Strange jigs to keep them from the floor,
Till they sink down and feel no more.

560   EPITAPH ON A PESSIMIST

I'm Smith of Stoke, aged sixty-odd,
    I've lived without a dame
From youth-time on: and would to God
    My dad had done the same.

(From the Greek Anthology)

I never cared for Life: Life cared for me,
And hence I owed it some fidelity.
It now says, "Cease; at length thou hast learnt to grind
Sufficient toll for an unwilling mind,
And I dismiss thee—not without regard
That thou didst ask no ill-advised reward,
Nor sought in me much more than thou couldst find."

CARDINAL BEMBO'S EPITAPH ON RAPHAEL

Here's one in whom Nature feared—faint at such vying—
Eclipse while he lived, and decease at his dying.

CHRISTMAS 1924

"Peace upon Earth!" was said. We sing it,
And pay a million priests to bring it.
After two thousand years of mass
We've got as far as poison gas.

EPITAPH FOR GEORGE MOORE

"No mortal man beneath the sky
Can write such English as can I.
They say it holds no thought my own.
What then, such perfection is not known."

Heap dustbins on him:
They'll not meet
The apex of his self-conceit.

GERARD MANLEY HOPKINS
1844–1889

565 BY MRS. HOPLEY, ON SEEING HER CHILDREN
SAY GOODNIGHT TO THEIR FATHER

> Bid your Papa Goodnight. Sweet exhibition!
> They kiss the Rod with filial submission.

566
> Of virtues I most warmly bless,
> Most rarely see, Unselfishness.
> And to put graver sins aside
> I own a preference for Pride.

? NORMAN DOUGLAS
1858–1962

567
> Il y avait un jeune homme de Dijon,
> Qui n'avait que peu de religion.
>> Il dit: "Quant à moi,
>> Je déteste tous les trois,
> Le Père, et le Fils, et le Pigeon."

EDWIN ARLINGTON ROBINSON
1859–1935

568   THE RAVEN

> The gloom of death is on the raven's wing,
>> The song of death is in the raven's cries:
> But when Demophilus begins to sing,
>> The raven dies.

(After the Greek of Nikarchos)

So now the very bones of you are gone
Where they were dust and ashes long ago;
And there was the last ribbon you tied on
To bind your hair, and that is dust also;
And somewhere there is dust that was of old
A soft and scented garment that you wore—
The same that once till dawn did closely fold
You in with fair Charaxus, fair no more.

But Sappho, and the white leaves of her song,
Will make your name a word for all to learn,
And all to love thereafter, even while
It's but a name; and this will be as long
As there are distant ships that will return
Again to Naucratis and to the Nile.

(After the Greek of Poseidippos)

LAIS TO APHRODITE* 570

When I, poor Lais, with my crown
Of beauty could laugh Hellas down,
Young lovers crowded at my door,
Where now my lovers come no more.

So, Goddess, you will not refuse
A mirror that has now no use;
For what I was I cannot be,
And what I am I will not see.

(After the Greek of Plato)

* For earlier versions see Nos. 70 and 221.

No dust have I to cover me,
    My grave may no man show;
My tomb is this unending sea,
    And I lie far below.
My fate, O stranger, was to drown;
And where it was the ship went down
    Is what the sea-birds know.

(After the Greek of Glaukos)

A. E. HOUSMAN
1859–1936

572   Here dead lie we because we did not choose
            To live and shame the land from which we sprung.
        Life, to be sure, is nothing much to lose;
            But young men think it is, and we were young.

573   Some can gaze and not be sick,
                But I could never learn the trick.
                There's this to say for blood and breath,
                They give a man a taste for death.

JOHN COLLINS BOSSIDY
1860–1928

574   I come from the city of Boston,
                    The home of the bean and the cod,
                Where the Lowells talk to the Cabots
                    And the Cabots talk only to God.

SIR W. A. RALEIGH
1861–1922

WISHES OF AN ELDERLY MAN 575

I wish I loved the Human Race;
I wish I loved its silly face;
I wish I liked the way it walks;
I wish I liked the way it talks;
And when I'm introduced to one
I wish I thought What Jolly Fun!

W. B. YEATS
1865–1939

TO A POET, WHO WOULD HAVE ME PRAISE 576
CERTAIN BAD POETS, IMITATORS OF HIS
AND MINE

You say, as I have often given tongue
In praise of what another's said or sung,
'Twere politic to do the like by these;
But was there ever dog that praised his fleas?

THE COMING OF WISDOM WITH TIME 577

Though leaves are many, the root is one;
Through all the lying days of my youth
I swayed my leaves and flowers in the sun;
Now I may wither into the truth.

TO BE CARVED ON A STONE AT THOR BALLYLEE

I, the poet William Yeats,
With old mill boards and sea-green slates,
And smithy work from the Gort forge,
Restored this tower for my wife George;
And may these characters remain
When all is ruin once again.

YOUTH AND AGE

Much did I rage when young,
Being by the world oppressed,
But now with flattering tongue
It speeds the parting guest.

THE NINETEENTH CENTURY AND AFTER

Though the great song return no more
There's keen delight in what we have:
The rattle of pebbles on the shore
Under the receding wave.

THREE MOVEMENTS

Shakespearean fish swam the sea, far away from land;
Romantic fish swam in nets coming to the hand;
What are all those fish that lie gasping on the strand?

Cast a cold eye
On life, on death.
Horseman, pass by!

ANONYMOUS
ON MIKE O'DAY   583

This is the grave of Mike O'Day
Who died maintaining his right of way.
His right was clear, his will was strong,
But he's just as dead as if he'd been wrong.

EPITAPH ON A DENTIST   584

Stranger, approach this spot with gravity;
John Brown is filling his last cavity.

J. K. STEPHEN
1859–1892
TO R. K.*   585

Will there never come a season
Which shall rid us from the curse
Of a prose which knows no reason
And an unmelodious verse:
When the world shall cease to wonder
At the genius of an Ass.
And a boy's eccentric blunder
Shall not bring success to pass:
            * Rudyard Kipling.

When mankind shall be delivered
From the clash of magazines,
And the inkstand shall be shivered
Into countless smithereens:
When there stands a muzzled stripling
Mute, beside a muzzled bore:
When the Rudyards cease from kipling
And the Haggards ride no more?

RUDYARD KIPLING
1865–1936
586   FROM "EPITAPHS OF THE WAR"

A SON

My son was killed while laughing at some jest. I would I knew
What it was, and it might serve me in a time when jests are few.

THE COWARD

I could not look on Death, which being known
Men led me to him, blindfold and alone.

THE REFINED MAN

I was of delicate mind. I stepped aside for my needs,
    Disdaining the common office. I was seen from afar and
    killed. . . .
How is this matter for mirth? Let each man be judged by his
    deeds.
    I have paid my price to live with myself on the terms that I willed.

COMMON FORM

If any question why we died,
Tell them, because our fathers lied.

A DEAD STATESMAN

I could not dig: I dared not rob:
Therefore I lied to please the mob.
Now all my lies are proved untrue
And I must face the men I slew.
What tale shall serve me here among
Mine angry and defrauded young?

A DRIFTER OFF TARENTUM

He from the wind-bitten north with ship and companions
    descended.
  Searching for eggs of death spawned by invisible hulls,
Many he found and drew forth. Of a sudden the fishery ended
  In flame and a clamorous breath not new to the eye-pecking
    gulls.

THE BRIDEGROOM

Call me not false, beloved,
    If, from thy scarce-known breast
So little time removed,
    In other arms I rest.

For this more ancient bride
    Whom coldly I embrace
Was constant at my side
    Before I saw thy face.

Our marriage, often set—
    By miracle delayed—
At last is consummate,
    And cannot be unmade.

Live, then, whom Life shall cure,
    Almost, of Memory,
And leave us to endure
    Its immortality.

587   ON THE ARMY OF SPARTANS WHO
DIED AT THERMOPYLAI

Tell them in Lakedaimon, passer-by,
We kept the Spartan code, and here we lie.

(After the Greek of Simonides)

EDGAR LEE MASTERS
1869–1950
588   EDITOR WHEDON

To be able to see every side of every question,
To be on every side, to be everything, to be nothing long;
To pervert truth, to ride it for a purpose,
To use great feelings and passions of the human family
For base designs, for cunning ends,
To wear a mask like the Greek actors—
Your eight-page paper—behind which you huddle,
Bawling through the megaphone of big type:
"This is I, the giant."
Thereby also living the life of a sneak-thief,
Poisoned with the anonymous words
Of your clandestine soul.
To scratch dirt over scandal for money,
And exhume it to the winds for revenge,
Or to sell papers,
Crushing reputations, or bodies, if need be,
To win at any cost save your own life.
To glory in demoniac power, ditching civilization,
As a paranoiac boy puts a log on the track
And derails the express train.

To be an editor, as I was.
Then to lie here close by the river over the place
Where the sewage flows from the village,
And the empty cans and garbage are dumped,
And abortions are hidden.

JUDGE SOMERS

How does it happen, tell me,
That I who was the most erudite of lawyers,
Who knew Blackstone and Coke
Almost by heart, who made the greatest speech
The court-house ever heard, and wrote
A brief that won the praise of Justice Breese—
How does it happen, tell me,
That I lie here unmarked, forgotten,
While Chase Henry, the town drunkard,
Has a marble block, topped by an urn,
Wherein Nature, in a mood ironical,
Has sown a flowering weed?

THE CIRCUIT JUDGE

Take note, passers-by, of the sharp erosions
Eaten in my head-stone by the wind and rain—
Almost as if an intangible Nemesis or hatred
Were marking scores against me,
But to destroy, and not preserve, my memory.
I in life was the Circuit Judge, a maker of notches,
Deciding cases on the points the lawyers scored,
Not on the right of the matter.
O wind and rain, leave my head-stone alone!

For worse than the anger of the wronged,
The curses of the poor,
Was to lie speechless, yet with vision clear,
Seeing that even Hod Putt, the murderer,
Hanged by my sentence,
Was innocent in soul compared with me.

HILAIRE BELLOC
1870–1956

591   ON NOMAN, A GUEST

Dear Mr. Noman, does it ever strike you,
The more we see of you, the less we like you?

592   LORD FINCHLEY

Lord Finchley tried to mend the Electric Light
Himself. It struck him dead: And serve him right!
It is the business of the wealthy man
To give employment to the artisan.

593   Here richly with ridiculous display
Killed by excess was Wormwood laid away,
While all of his acquaintance sneered and slanged,
I wept: for I had longed to see him hanged.

                              (*After the French of Malherbe*)

ON A GENERAL ELECTION

The accursed power which stands on Privilege
(And goes with Women, and Champagne and Bridge)
Broke—and Democracy resumed her reign:
(Which goes with Bridge, and Women and Champagne).

ON HIS BOOKS

When I am dead, I hope it may be said:
"His sins were scarlet, but his books were read."

THE FALSE HEART

I said to Heart, "How goes it?" Heart replied,
"Right as a Ribstone Pippin!" But it lied.

EPITAPH

Ci gît celui qui t'aimait trop
Pour ton bonheur et son repos.

First in his pride the orient sun's display   598
Renews the world, and changes night to day.
A little later—round about eleven—
Juliet appears, and changes earth to heaven.

Lauda tu Ilarion audacem et splendidum,★
Who was always beginning things and never ended 'em.

600   ON A PURITAN

He served his God so faithfully and well
That now he sees him face to face, in hell.

601   ON A SUNDIAL

I am a sundial, and I make a botch
Of what is done far better by a watch.

602   ON ANOTHER

I am a sundial, turned the wrong way round.
I cost my foolish mistress fifty pound.

603   ON ANOTHER

I am a sundial. Ordinary words
Cannot express my thoughts on birds.

604   ON MUNDANE ACQUAINTANCES

Good morning, Algernon: Good morning, Percy.
Good morning, Mrs. Roebeck. Christ have mercy!
★ Praise Hilaire the bold and brilliant.

I curse my bearing, childhood, youth,   605
I curse the sea, sun, mountains, moon,
I curse my learning, search for truth,
I curse the dawning, night, and noon.

Cold, joyless I will live, though clean,
Nor, by my marriage, mould to earth
Young lives to see what I have seen,
To curse—as I have cursed—their birth.

ON AN ANNIVERSARY   606
AFTER READING THE DATES IN A BOOK
OF LYRICS

With Fifteen-ninety or Sixteen-sixteen
We end Cervantes, Marot, Nashe or Green:
Then Sixteen-thirteen till two score and nine,
Is Crashaw's niche, that honey-lipped divine.
And so when all my little work is done
They'll say I came in Eighteen-seventy-one,
And died in Dublin. . . . What year will they write
For my poor passage to the stall of Night?

THE PASSING OF THE SHEE
AFTER LOOKING AT ONE OF A.E.'S PICTURES

Adieu, sweet Angus, Maeve and Fand,
Ye plumed yet skinny Shee
Our poets walked with hand in hand
To learn fine ecstasy.

We've learned to cherish Kerry men,
The ditches lovers know,
The badger, salmon, water hen,
The weazel, lark and crow.

EPITAPH
AFTER READING RONSARD'S LINES FROM
RABELAIS

If fruits are fed on any beast
Let vine-roots suck this parish priest,
For while he lived, no summer sun
Went up but he'd a bottle done,
And in the starlight beer and stout
Kept his waistcoat bulging out.

Then Death that changes happy things
Damned his soul to water springs.

A WISH

May seven tears in every week
Touch the hollow of your cheek,
That I—signed with such a dew—
For a lion's share may sue
Of the roses ever curled
Round the May-pole of the world.

Heavy riddles lie in this,
Sorrow's sauce for every kiss.

THE CURSE

To a sister of an enemy of the author's who disapproved of
"The Playboy"

Lord, confound this surly sister,
Blight her brow with blotch and blister,
Cramp her larynx, lung, and liver,
In her guts a galling give her.
Let her live to earn her dinners
In Mountjoy with seedy sinners:
Lord, this judgment quickly bring,
And I'm your servant, J. M. Synge.

I read about the Blaskets and Dunquin,
The Wicklow towns and fair days I've been in.
I read of Galway, Mayo, Aranmore,
And men with kelp along a wintry shore.
Then I remembered that that "I" was I,
And I'd a filthy job—to waste and die.

STEPHEN CRANE
1871–1900

612   In the desert
I saw a creature, naked, bestial,
Who, squatting upon the ground,
Held his heart in his hands,
And ate of it.
I said, "Is it good, friend?"
"It is bitter—bitter," he answered;
"But I like it
Because it is bitter,
And because it is my heart."

613   A man said to the universe:
"Sir, I exist!"
"However," replied the universe,
"The fact has not created in me
A sense of obligation."

MAX BEERBOHM
1872–1956

614   ELEGY ON ANY LADY
BY
GEORGE MOORE

That she adored me as the most
Adorable of males
I think I may securely boast,
Dead women tell no tales.

I met Musette
In the water-closet—
Or if it wasn't there, where *was* it?
And let me see:
Was it not Mimi
That made such passionate love to me
In the W.C.?
Which *was* it?

EPITAPH FOR G. B. SHAW   616

I strove with all, for all were worth my strife.
   Nature I loathed, and, next to Nature, Art.
I chilled both feet on the thin ice of Life.
   It broke, and I emit one final fart.

ADDITION TO KIPLING'S   617
"THE DEAD KING (EDWARD VII), 1910"

Wisely and well was it said of him, "Hang it all, he's a
Mixture of Jesus, Apollo, Goliath and Julius Caesar!"
Always he plans as an ever Do-Right-Man, never an Err-man,
And never a drop of the blood in his beautiful body was German.
"God save him," we said when he lived, but the words now
   sound odd,
For we know that in Heaven above at this moment *he's* saving
   God.

ROBERT FROST
1875–1963

618   FIRE AND ICE

        Some say the world will end in fire,
        Some say in ice.
        From what I've tasted of desire
        I hold with those who favor fire.
        But if it had to perish twice,
        I think I know enough of hate
        To say that for destruction ice
        Is also great
        And would suffice.

WALTER DE LA MARE
1873–1956

619   SUSANNAH PROUT

            Here lies my wife,
            Susannah Prout;
            She was a shrew
            I don't misdoubt:
            Yet all I have
            I'd give, could she
            But for one hour
            Come back to me.

Three sisters rest beneath
This cypress shade,
Sprightly Rebecca, Anne,
And Adelaide.
Gentle their hearts to all
On earth, save Man;
In Him, they said, all Grief,
All Wo began.
Spinsters they lived, and spinsters
Here are laid;
Sprightly Rebecca, Anne,
And Adelaide.

THOMAS LOGGE   621

Here lies Thomas Logge—A Rascally Dogge;
A poor useless creature—by choice as by nature;
Who never served God—for kindness or Rod;
Who, for pleasure or penny,—never did any
Work in his life—but to marry a Wife,
And live aye in strife:
And all this he says—at the end of his days
Lest some fine canting pen
Should be at him again.

A Shepherd, Ned Vaughan,
'Neath this Tombstone do bide,
His Crook in his hand,
And his Dog him beside.
Bleak and cold fell the Snow
On Marchmallysdon Steep,
And folded both sheepdog
And Shepherd in Sleep.

623   CORPORAL PYM

This quiet mound beneath
    Lies Corporal Pym.
He had no fear of death;
    Nor Death of him.

624   SLIM CUNNING HANDS

Slim cunning hands at rest, and cozening eyes—
Under this stone one loved too wildly lies;
How false she was, no granite could declare;
    Nor all earth's flowers how fair.

JOHN MASEFIELD
1878–1967

AN EPILOGUE   625

I have seen flowers come in stony places
And kind things done by men with ugly faces,
And the gold cup won by the worst horse at the races,
So I trust, too.

OLIVER ST. JOHN GOGARTY
1878–1957

ON THE USE OF JAYSHUS   626

The plainer Dubliners amaze us
By their so frequent use of "Jayshus!"
Which makes me entertain the notion
It is not always from devotion.

TO DEATH   627

But for your Terror
Where would be Valour?
What is Love for
    But to stand in your way?
Taker and Giver,
For all your endeavour
You leave us with more
    Than you touch with decay.

Only the Lion and the Cock,
As Galen says, withstand Love's shock,
So, Dearest, do not think me rude
If I yield now to lassitude,
But sympathise with me, I know
You would not have me roar, or crow.

VACHEL LINDSAY
1879–1931

629   THE LEADEN-EYED

Let not young souls be smothered out before
They do quaint deeds and fully flaunt their pride.
It is the world's one crime its babes grow dull,
Its poor are ox-like, limp and leaden-eyed.

Not that they starve, but starve so dreamlessly,
Not that they sow, but that they seldom reap,
Not that they serve, but have no gods to serve,
Not that they die but that they die like sheep.

630   WHAT THE MOON SAW

Two statesmen met by moonlight.
Their ease was partly feigned.
They glanced about the prairie.
Their faces were constrained.
In various ways aforetime
They had misled the state,
Yet did it so politely
Their henchmen thought them great.

They sat beneath a hedge and spake
No word, but had a smoke.
A satchel passed from hand to hand.
Next day, the deadlock broke.

MARTIN ARMSTRONG
1882–1974

TO A JILT   631

Girl, when rejecting me you never guessed
I gave you all the beauty you possessed.
Now that I've ceased to love you, you remain
As once, a creature singularly plain.

JAMES JOYCE
1882–1941

⟨ON LADY GREGORY'S SEARCH   632
FOR TALENT⟩

There was a kind Lady called Gregory,
Said, "Come to me, poets in beggary,"
    But found her imprudence
    When thousands of students
Cried "All we are in that catégory!"

633   when any mortal(even the most odd)

can justify the ways of man to God
i'll think it strange that normal mortals can

not justify the ways of God to man

634   for prodigal read generous
—for youth read age—
read for sheer wonder mere surprise
(then turn the page)

contentment read for ecstasy
—for poem prose—
caution for curiosity
(and close your eyes)

635   mr u will not be missed
who as an anthologist
sold the many on the few
not excluding mr u

636   a politician is an arse upon
which everyone has sat except a man

love is a place 637
& through this place of
love move
(with brightness of peace)
all places

yes is a world
& in this world of
yes live
(skilfully curled)
all worlds

IN) 638
all those who got
athlete's mouth jumping
on&off bandwagons
(MEMORIAM

slightly before the middle of Congressman Pudd 639
's 4th of July oration, with a curse and a frown
Amy Lowell got up
and all the little schoolchildren sat down

W. N. EWER
1885–1977
HOW ODD 640

How odd
Of God
To choose
The Jews.

D. H. LAWRENCE
1885–1930

641   O! START A REVOLUTION

O! start a revolution, somebody!
not to get the money
but to lose it all for ever.

O! start a revolution, somebody!
not to install the working classes
but to abolish the working classes for ever
and have a world of men.

642   THE MOSQUITO KNOWS—

The mosquito knows full well, small as he is
he's a beast of prey.
But after all
he only takes his bellyful,
he doesn't put my blood in the bank.

643   DESIRE IS DEAD

Desire may be dead
and still a man can be
a meeting place for sun and rain,
wonder outwaiting pain
as in a wintry tree.

Everything that lives has its own proper pride
as a columbine flower has, or even a starling walking and
   looking around

And the base things like hyaenas or bed-bugs have least
   pride of being,
they are humble, with a creeping humility, being parasites
   or carrion creatures.

FOOD OF THE NORTH   645

The food of the north tastes too much of the fat
   of the pig
fat of the pig!

Take me south again, to the olive trees
and oil me with the lymph of silvery trees,
oil me with the lymph of trees
not with the fat of the pig.

LORD TENNYSON AND LORD MELCHETT   646

"Dost tha hear my horse's feet, as he canters away?
Property! Property! Property! that's what they seem to say!"

Do you hear my Rolls Royce purr, as it glides away?
—I lick the cream off property! that's what it seems to say!

"GROSS, COARSE, HIDEOUS"
(POLICE DESCRIPTION OF MY PICTURES)

Lately I saw a sight most quaint:
London's lily-like policemen faint
in virgin outrage as they viewed
the nudity of a Lawrence nude!

FLOWERS AND MEN

Flowers achieve their own floweriness and it is a miracle.
Men don't achieve their own manhood, alas, oh alas! alas!

All I want of you, men and women,
All I want of you
is that you shall achieve your beauty
as the flowers do.

Oh leave off saying I want you to be savages.
Tell me, is the gentian savage, at the top of its coarse stem?
Oh what in you can answer to this blueness?

I want you to be as savage as the gentian and the daffodil.
Tell me! Tell me! is there in you a beauty to compare
to the honeysuckle at evening now
pouring out its breath.

DEAN INGE   649

Hark! the herald angels sing
timidly, because Dean Inge
has arrived, and seems to be
bored with immortality.

D. H. LAWRENCE AND JAMES JOYCE   650

Lawrence here for ever blames
Joyce's reticence, while James
goes on stating his abhorrence
of the prudery of Lawrence.

You cannot hope   651
    to bribe or twist,
thank God! the
    British journalist.

But, seeing what
    the man will do
unbribed, there's
    no occasion to.

HILAIRE BELLOC   652

Here lies Hilaire Belloc, who
preferred the devil to a Jew.
Now he has his chance to choose
between the devil and the Jews.

653 TRANSLATOR TO TRANSLATED

O Harry Heine, curses be,
I live too late to sup with thee!
Who can demolish at such polished ease
Philistia's pomp and Art's pomposities!

654

I dreamt that I was God Himself
Whom heavenly joy immerses,
And all the angels sat about
And praised my verses.

(After the German of Heine)

655 MR. HOUSMAN'S MESSAGE

O woe, woe,
People are born and die,
We also shall be dead pretty soon
Therefore let us act as if we were
dead already.

The bird sits on the hawthorn tree
But he dies also, presently.
Some lads get hung, and some get shot.
Woeful is the human lot.
Woe! woe, etcetera....

London is a woeful place,
Shropshire is much pleasanter.

Then let us smile a little space
Upon fond nature's morbid grace.

           Oh, Woe, woe, woe, etcetera. . . .

MARIANNE MOORE
b. 1887

Poetry   656

I, too, dislike it.
   Reading it, however, with a perfect contempt for it, one
      discovers in
   it, after all, a place for the genuine.

SIR GEORGE ROSTREVOR HAMILTON
1888–1967

TO THE GREEK ANTHOLOGISTS   657

   As tongueless Echo in the pastoral vale
   Repeats the music of the nightingale,
   So may I catch some wood-notes of your song
   And in sweet-vowelled English echo them along.

                  (After the Greek of Satyros)

EXILE   658

   I left the farm I loved. I went
      To merchant in a foreign town:
   To yet more fatal banishment
      I with the ship went down.

O tempest, never have I seen
   A thing so cruel on the land:
At home the very graves are green,
   And I lie in the sand.

(After the Greek of Isidoros of Aigai)

659   EXCHANGE

Finding gold, *A* left
   A rope upon the ground:
B, of the gold bereft,
   Swung in the rope he found.

(After the Greek of Plato)

660   THE OLD OX

Not to the butcher did he pass,
   This good old ox, with labour spent:
Knee-deep he stands in meadow-grass,
   Deep-lowing for his deep content.

(After the Greek of Addaios of Makedon)

661   SCHOOLMASTER

All the world's a school.
   To save it from disaster,
I bear viceregent rule
   For God, the great Headmaster.

A man of independent means—
That means that I depend
Only on those whom work demeans:
So be it, without end!

EDITH BONE
1889–1975

ON MYSELF 663

Here lies the body of Edith Bone.
All her life she lived alone,
Until Death added the final S
And put an end to her loneliness.

IVOR GURNEY
1890–1937

REQUIEM 664

Pour out your light, O stars, and do not hold
    Your loveliest shining from earth's outworn shell—
Pure and cold your radiance, pure and cold
    My dead friend's face as well.

EPITAPH ON A YOUNG CHILD 665

They will bury that fair body and cover you—
You shall no more be seen of the eyes of men,
Not again shall you search the woodlands—not ever again
For violets—the wind shall be no more dear lover of you.

Other children shall grow as fair, but not so dear.
And the cold spirited shall say "It is wrong that the body
Should be so beautiful"—O puritans warped to moody!
You were the true darling of the earth of your shire.

And all the flowers you touched, but would for pity not pick,
In the next Spring shall regret you and on and so on—
Whether you are born again your love shall not be done—
In the most wonderful April or October your spirit shall be
    mystic.

Dear body (it is an evil age), that so enclosed
So lovely a spirit, generous, quick to another's small pain:
Is it true you in the dark earth must be down-lain?
Are there no more smiles from you in the house, sunlight drowsed?

I must find out a love to console my hurt loneliness,
Forget your children's beauty in the conflict of days—
Until there come to me also the sweetness of some boy's
Or girl's beauty—a Western spirit in a loved coloured dress of
    flesh.

COLIN ELLIS
1895–1969
666   BUNGALOID GROWTH

        When England's multitudes observed with frowns
            That those who came before had spoiled the towns,
        "This can no longer be endured!" they cried,
            And set to work to spoil the countryside.

Adder, whose art condenses and refines
The malice of three volumes in two lines,
Is still dissatisfied, and racks his head
To say things better that were best not said.

ON A GENTLEMAN MARRYING HIS COOK 668

Though to good breeding she made no pretence,
She had good looks, good nature, and good sense:
Would that men's wives were all of them good cooks,
And had good sense, good nature, and good looks.

INTERNATIONAL CONFERENCE 669

To kill its enemies and cheat its friends,
Each nation its prerogative defends;
Yet some their efforts for goodwill maintain,
In hope, in faith, in patience, and in vain.

THE MODERN WORLD 670

Science finds out ingenious ways to kill
Strong men, and keep alive the weak and ill,
That these a sickly progeny many breed
Too poor to tax, too numerous to feed.

J. B. MORTON
b. 1893

671   EPITAPH

A glassblower lies here at rest
Who one day burst his noble chest
While trying, in a fit of malice,
To blow a second Crystal Palace.

672   EPITAPH

Tread softly; bid a solemn music sound;
Here in a little plot of English ground
Lies Smudge, who sold us medicated beer,
And double-crossed his friends, and died a peer.

673   Let poets praise the softer winds of spring,
                The clearer skies, the magic-laden air;
           I mark the season by a greater thing—
                Lady Cabstanleigh's back in Berkeley Square.

ROBERT GRAVES
b. 1895

674   THE THREE-FACED

Who calls her two-faced? Faces, she has three:
The first inscrutable, for the outer world;
The second shrouded in self-contemplation;
The third, her face of love,
Once for an endless moment turned on me.

TWINS

Siamese twins: one, maddened by
The other's moral bigotry,
Resolved at length to misbehave
And drink them both into the grave.

IN TIME

In time all undertakings are made good,
All cruelties remedied,
Each bond resealed more firmly than before—
Befriend us, Time, Love's gaunt executor!

VARIABLES OF GREEN

Grass-green and aspen-green,
Laurel-green and sea-green,
Fine-emerald-green,
And many another hue:
As green commands the variables of green
So love my loves of you.

THE SHARP RIDGE

Since now I dare not ask
Any gift from you, or gentle task,
Or lover's promise—nor yet refuse
Whatever I can give and you dare choose—
Have pity on us both: choose well
On this sharp ridge dividing death from hell.

THE NARROW SEA

With you for mast and sail and flag,
And anchor never known to drag,
Death's narrow but oppressive sea
Looks not unnavigable to me.

680   LOVE WITHOUT HOPE

Love without hope, as when the young bird-catcher
Swept off his tall hat to the Squire's own daughter,
So let the imprisoned larks escape and fly
Singing about her head, as she rode by.

681   LOVERS IN WINTER

The posture of the tree
    Shows the prevailing wind;
And ours, long misery
    When you are long unkind.

But forward, look, we lean—
    Not backward as in doubt—
And still with branches green
    Ride our ill weather out.

682   UNDER THE POT

Sulkily the sticks burn, and though they crackle
    With scorn under the bubbling pot, or spout
Magnanimous jets of flame against the smoke,
    At each heel and a dirty sap breaks out.

Confess, creatures, how sulkily ourselves
   We hiss with doom, fuel of a sodden age—
Not rapt up roaring to the chimney stack
   On incandescent clouds of spirit or rage.

TILTH   683

("Robert Graves, the British veteran, is no longer in the poetic
swim. He still resorts to traditional metres and rhyme, and to
such outdated words as *tilth*; witholding his 100% approbation
also from contemporary poems that favour sexual freedom."

(From a New York critical weekly)

   Gone are the drab monosyllabic days
   When "agricultural labour" still was *tilth*;
   And "100% approbation", *praise*;
   And "pornographic modernism", *filth*—
   Yet still I stand by *tilth* and *filth* and *praise*.

REPROACH TO JULIA   684

   Julia, how Irishly you sacrifice
   Love to pity, pity to ill-humour,
   Yourself to love, still haggling at the price.

THE EUGENIST   685

Come, human dogs, interfertilitate—
   Blackfellows and white lord, brown, yellow and red!
Accept the challenge of the lately bred
   Newfoundland terrier with the dachshund gait.

Breed me gigantic pygmies, meek-eyed Scots,
    Phlegmatic Irish, perfume-hating Poles,
Poker-faced, toothy, pigtailed Hottentots,
    And Germans with no envy in their souls.

686   POETS' CORNER
              De ambobus mundis ille
              Convoravit diligens. . . .★

The Best of Both Worlds being Got
Between th'Evangel and the Pot,
He, though Exorbitantly Vice'd,
Had Re-discover'd Thirst for Christ
And Fell a Victim (Young as This),
To Ale, God's Love and Syphilis.

Here then in Triumph See Him Stand,
Laurels for Halo, Scroll in Hand,
Whyle Ganymeds and Cherubim
And Squabby Nymphs Rejoyce with Him:
Aye, Scroll Shall Fall and Laurels Fade
Long, Long before his Debts are Pay'd.

687   EPITAPH ON AN UNFORTUNATE ARTIST

He found a formula for drawing comic rabits:
    The formula for drawing comic rabbits paid,
So in the end he could not change the tragic habits
    This formula for drawing comic rabbits made.

★ He ate greedily and diligently of both worlds.

AT FIRST SIGHT 688

"Love at first sight", some say, misnaming
Discovery of twinned helplessness
Against the huge tug of procreation.

But friendship at first sight? This also
Catches fiercely at the surprised heart
So that the cheek blanches and then blushes.

THE WEATHER OF OLYMPUS 689

Zeus was once overheard to shout at Hera:
   "You hate it, do you? Well, I hate it worse—
East wind in May, sirocco all the Summer.
   Hell take this whole impossible Universe!"

A scholiast explains his warm rejoinder,
   Which sounds too man-like for Olympic use,
By noting that the snake-tailed Chthonian winds
   Were answerable to Fate alone, not Zeus.

EDMUND BLUNDEN
1896–1974

THE DOG FROM MALTA 690

He came from Malta, and Eumelus says
He had no dog like him in all his days;
We called him Bull; he went into the dark;
Along those roads we cannot hear him bark.

(After the Greek of Tymnes)

691   EPITAPH

Nor practising virtue nor committing crime,
So busily he left those things undone
He should not do, that he had never time
Of all the things he should do, to do one.

692   ENGLISH LIBERAL

"I think," thought Sam Butler,
        "Truth ever lies
        In mean compromise."
What could be subtler
Than the thought of Sam Butler?

693   ADMONITION TO THE MUSE

Yes Miss
Put up your pretty little mouth for a kiss
But remember this
Poetry may deal with knowledge or imagination fact or fiction
But to cleanse that Augean stable we've got to pitch poetic
    thought after poetic diction
So run along now to your chamber Miss and rhyme with bliss.

CRUEL CLEVER CAT

Sally, having swallowed cheese,
Directs down holes the scented breeze,
Enticing thus with bated breath.
Nice mice to an untimely death.

GENTLEMEN

The flower of the race—
Shall I not then, on entering
This subterraneous building,
This suite of dazzling whiteness,
Bare my head in reverence?
Is this not too a temple,
A Holy Place?

ROY CAMPBELL
1902–1957

FISHING BOATS IN MARTIGUES

Around the quays, kicked off in twos
The Four Winds dry their wooden shoes.

ON SOME SOUTH AFRICAN NOVELISTS

You praise the firm restraint with which they write—
I'm with you there, of course:
They use the snaffle and the curb all right,
But where's the bloody horse?

698 *QUAND ON N'A PAS CE QUE L'ON AIME,*
    IL FAUT AIMER CE QUE L'ON A—

Cold as no love, and wild with all negation—
Oh Death in Life, the lack of animation.

699   TO SCHOOL!

Let all the little poets be gathered together in classes
And let prizes be given to them by the Prize Asses
And let them be sure to call all the little poets young
And worse follow what's bad begun
But do not expect the Muse to attend this school
Why look already how far off she has flown, she is no fool.

700   DEAR FEMALE HEART

Dear Female Heart, I am sorry for you,
You must suffer, that is all you can do.
But if you like, in common with the rest of the human race,
You may also look most absurd with a miserable face.

701   REVERSIONARY

The Lion dishonoured bids death come,
The worm in like hap lingers on.
The Lion dead, his pride no less,
The world inherits wormliness.

This Englishwoman is so refined
She has no bosom and no behind.

KENNETH REXROTH
b. 1905

⟨FROM THE PERSIAN⟩ 703

Naked out of the dark we came.
Naked into the dark we go.
Come to my arms, naked in the dark.

ANONYMOUS

SOLDIERS 704

Soldiers who wish to be a hero
Are practically zero,
But those who wish to be civilians,
Jesus, they run into millions.

FROM A LAVATORY WALL 705

Above:
Wise men come here to shit,
And fools come here to show their wit.

Below:
By writing this, you bleeding arse,
You include yourself in the latter class.

706   FROM A WOMAN TO A GREEDY LOVER

What is this recompense you'd have from me?
Melville asked no compassion of the sea.
Roll to and fro, forgotten in my wrack,
Love as you please—I owe you nothing back.

707   FORGIVE ME, SIRE

Forgive me, Sire, for cheating your intent,
That I, who should command a regiment,
Do amble amiably here, O God,
One of the neat ones in your awkward squad.

708   LAST YEAR'S DISCUSSION: THE NOBEL
RUSSIAN

In Fond du Lac, Bronxville, Butte, Chicago,
Everyone ordered Dr. Zhivago,
A novel by Boris Pasternak.

But how many read it from front to back
In Bronxville, Chicago, Butte, Fond du Lac?

Coquettes with doctors; hoards her breath
  For blandishments; fluffs out her hair;
And keeps her stubborn suitor, Death,
  Moping upon the stair.

THE MUTED SCREEN OF GRAHAM GREENE 710

Were all our sins so empty of enjoyment,
All sinners gloomy as the ones he paints,
The Devil soon, I think, would lack employment
And the earth teem with saints.

SQUEEZE PLAY 711

Jackson Pollock had a quaint
Way of saying to his sibyl,
"Shall I dribble?
Should I paint?"
And with never an instant's quibble,
Sibyl always answered,
"Dribble".

THE ADVERSARY 712

A mother's hardest to forgive,
Life is the fruit she longs to hand you,
Ripe on a plate. And while you live,
Relentlessly she understands you.

THE INDEPENDENT

So open was his mind, so wide
To welcome winds from every side
That public weather took dominion,
Sweeping him bare of all opinion.

THE DEMAGOGUE

That trumpet tongue which taught a nation
Loud lessons in vituperation
Teaches it yet another, viz.:
How sweet the noise of silence is.

GEOFFREY GRIGSON
b. 1905

714 AN ADMINISTRATOR

Tom Sucklebat, in dressing-gown, without his teeth,
    Appears a nasty kind of beeth,
But properly dressed, and with his button-holing smile,
    The merely nasty alters into vile.

715 ON A LOVER OF BOOKS

I

Clichés with worn wit combined
From the old clothes shop of his mind,
Shake out their moth when Vincent chatters,
And chatters on, of pointless matters.

Pull the chain,
   And Vincent's talk goes down the drain.
O pull the chain,
   And let the tank fill up again.

CRITICS AND POETS   716

Church Mouse commends: tapeworms and slugs grow wings,
Eels sneak from sludge and think on higher things.
Gut, Gland, Snitch and Martin Tupper
Sit down, with Shakespeare, to a P.E.N. Club supper.

ON THE RELINQUISHMENT OF A TITLE   717

Lords have been made whose hired robes have hidden
A life of treading in the dirtiest midden.
This lord, whose hopes and head were both too big,
Discarded ermine to reveal a pig.

W. H. AUDEN
1907–1974

LOST   718

Lost on a fogbound spit of sand
In shoes that pinched me, close at hand
I heard the plash of Charon's oar,
Who ferries no one to a happy shore.

Some thirty inches from my nose
The frontier of my Person goes,
And all the untilled air between
Is private *pagus* or demesne.
Stranger, unless with bedroom eyes
I beckon you to fraternize,
Beware of rudely crossing it:
I have no gun, but I can spit.

720   Private faces in public places
Are wiser and nicer
Than public faces in private places.

THEODORE ROETHKE
1908–1963

721   ACADEMIC

The stethoscope tells what everyone fears:
Your'e likely to go on living for years,
With a nurse-maid waddle and a shop-girl simper,
And the style of your prose growing limper and limper.

RICHARD USBORNE
b. 1910

722   EPITAPH ON A PARTY GIRL

Lovely Pamela, who found
One sure way to get around
Goes to bed beneath this stone
Early, sober, and alone.

FROM THE EPIGRAMS OF MARTIAL

I

Laid with papyrus to catch fire
And lightly heaped, the funeral pyre
Was all prepared, the wife was buying
Myrrh and cinnamon, and crying,
The grave, the bier, the corpse-perfumer
Were ready, when the dying Numa
Declared his previous will invalid,
Named me his heir—and promptly rallied.

II

Whenever you drink all night you make
Huge promises, which next day you break.
Booze in the morning—for *my* sake.

III

Garland of roses, whether you come
From Tiber or from Tusculum,
Whether the earth you splashed with red
Was Paestum's or the flower-bed
Of some Praeneste farmer's wife
Who snipped you with her gardening-knife,
No matter in which countryside
You flew your flag before you died.—
To lend my gift an added charm,
Let *him* believe you're from my farm.

IV

⟨EPITAPH FOR EROTION⟩
Here, six years old, by Destiny's crime
Made a ghost before her time,

Erotion lies. Whoever you be,
Next lord of my small property,
See that the dues of death are paid
Annually to her slender shade:
So may your hearth burn bright and strong,
Your household thrive, yourself live long,
And this small stone, throughout the years,
Remain your only cause for tears.

V

Either get out of the house or conform to my tastes, woman.
I'm no strait-laced Roman.
I like prolonging the nights agreeably with wine: you, after one
    glass of water,
Rise and retire with an air of hauteur.
You prefer darkness: I enjoy love-making
With a witness—a lamp shining or the dawn breaking.
You wear bed-jackets, tunics, thick woollen stuff,
Whereas I think no woman on her back can ever be naked
    enough.
I love girls who kiss like doves and hang round my neck:
You give me the sort of peck
Due to your grandmother as a morning salute.
In bed, you're motionless, mute—
Not a wriggle,
Not a giggle—
As solemn as a priestess at a shrine
Proffering incense and pure wine.
Yet every time Andromache went for a ride
In Hector's room, the household slaves used to masturbate
    outside;
Even modest Penelope, when Ulysses snored,
Kept her hand on the sceptre of her lord.
You refuse to be buggered; but it's a known fact

That Gracchus', Pompey's and Brutus' wives were willing
    partners in the act,
And that before Ganymede mixed Jupiter his tasty bowl
Juno filled the dear boy's role.
If you want to be uptight—all right,
By all means play Lucretia by day. But I need a Laïs at night.

ADRIAN MITCHELL
b. 1932

RIDDLE   724

Their tongues are knives, their forks are hands and feet.
They feed each other through their skins and eat
Religiously the spiced, symbolic meat.
The loving oven cooks them in its heat—
Two curried lovers on a rice-white sheet.

PRIVATE TRANSPORT   725

Round and round
His private roundabout
Drives the little critic's car—
A sneer on four square wheels

CELIA CELIA   726

When I am sad and weary,
When I think all hope has gone,
When I walk along High Holborn
I think of you with nothing on.

727   BOOK REVIEW

Longest and much the dearest—
The price of books benumbs—
With a slap of sail and a following gale
The rhymer Causley comes.

Now Causley comes from Cornwall,
And, brother, how it shows.
The harbour bell and that fishy smell
Assault both ears and nose.

But Causley's balladeering
Is good for youth to gnaw on
(In fact, to be frank, it's a Doggerel Bank
That any kid can draw on).

He uses simply, sociably
The skill he's been allotted;
And that's a start. Because in art
Not all the cream is clotted.

Acknowledgements

For permission to reprint copyright material, the following acknowledgements are made:

For lines by Martin Armstrong, to Messrs. A. D. Peters & Co. Ltd.
  from *54 Conceits*, 1933, Secker & Warburg
    To a Jilt

For lines by W. H. Auden, to Messrs. Faber & Faber Ltd. and
      Random House, Inc.
  from (a) *About the House*, Faber
    Lost; *Some Thirty Inches from my nose*
  from (b) *Collected Shorter Poems*, Faber
    Private faces in public places

For lines by Max Beerbohm, to the author and Messrs. William
      Heinemann Ltd.
  from *Max in Verse*, ed. J. G. Riewald, Heinemann.
    Vague Lyric by G.M.; Epitaph for G. B. Shaw; Addition to
    Kipling's "Dead King"; Elegy on any Lady by George Moore

For lines by Hilaire Belloc, to Messrs. A. D. Peters & Co. Ltd.
  from *Sonnets & Verse*, Duckworth
    On Noman; Lord Finchley; *Here richly with ridiculous display*;
    On a General Election; On his Books; The False Heart;
    Epitaph (*Ci gît . . .*); *First in his pride . . .*; Epitaph upon himself
    (*Lauda tu Ilarion . . .*); On a Puritan; On Mundane Acquaint-
    ances; *I am a sundial, and I make a botch*; *I am a sundial, turned the
    wrong way . . .*; *I am a sundial. Ordinary words.*

For lines by Edmund Blunden, to Messrs. A. D. Peters & Co. Ltd·
    The Dog from Malta

For lines by Norman Cameron, to Mr. Alan Hodge and The
      Hogarth Press.
  from *Collected Poems*, Hogarth Press
    From a Woman to a Greedy Lover; Forgive me, Sire

For lines by Roy Campbell, to The Bodley Head and to Curtis Brown, Ltd.
  from *Collected Poems*, Bodley Head
    Fishing Boats in Martigues; On some South African Novelists

For lines by e.e. cummings, to Messrs. MacGibbon & Kee Ltd./ Granada Publishing Ltd.
  from *Complete Poems*, MacGibbon & Kee/Granada
    when any mortal; for prodigal read generous; mr u will not be missed; a politician is an arse upon; love is a place; all those who got; slightly before the middle of Congressman Pudd

For lines by Russell Davies, to Messrs. A. D. Peters & Co. Ltd.
  from Review of Charles Causley, New Statesman

For lines by Walter de la Mare, to the Literary Trustees of Walter de la Mare and The Society of Authors as their representative.
  from *The Complete Poems of Walter de la Mare 1969*, Faber
    Susannah Prout; Three Sisters; Thomas Logge; Ned Vaughan; Corporal Pym; Slim Cunning Hands

For lines by Norman Douglas, to Messrs. Blond & Briggs
  Il y avait un jeune homme de Dijon

For lines by Colin Ellis★
  Bungaloid Growth; Adder's Epigrams; On a Gentleman marrying his cook; International Conference; The Modern World

For lines by W. N. Ewer★
  How odd

For lines by Robert Frost, to the Estate of Robert Frost, Mr. Edward Connery Lathem, Messrs. Jonathan Cape Ltd. and Messrs. Holt, Rinehart and Winston
  from *The Poetry of Robert Frost*, Jonathan Cape
    Fire and Ice

For lines by Oliver St. John Gogarty, to Mr. Oliver D. Gogarty, Messrs. Constable & Co. Ltd. and the Hutchinson Publishing Group Limited
  from *The Collected Poems of Oliver St. John Gogarty*, 1951, Constable
    To Death; After Galen
  from *As I was Going Down Sackville Street*
    The plainer Dubliners amaze us

For lines by Robert Graves, to the author
from *The Collected Poems, 1975*, Cassell
The Three-faced; Twins; In Time; Variables of Green; The
Sharp Ridge; The Narrow Sea; Love without Hope; Lovers in
Winter; Under the Pot; Tilth; At First Sight; The Weather
of Olympus

from *Poems 1953*
Reproach to Julia
from *The Collected Poems 1938–45*
The Eugenist
from *Poems 1955*
Poets' Corner
from *On English Poetry 1922*, Heinemann
Epitaph on an Unfortunate Artist

For lines by Ivor Gurney, to the Literary Estate of Ivor Gurney
and Messrs. Chatto & Windus
from *Poems of Ivor Gurney*, 1973, Chatto
Requiem; Epitaph on a Young Child

For lines by Sir G. R. Hamilton, to the author and Messrs. William
Heinemann Ltd.   from *Epigrams*, Heinemann
To the Greek Anthologists; Exile; Exchange; The Old Ox;
Schoolmaster; No Occupation

For lines by Thomas Hardy, to the Trustees of the Hardy Estate
and Macmillan, London and Basingstoke
from *Complete Poems*, Macmillan
Epitaph on a Pessimist; Epitaph (*I never cared for Life*);
Cardinal Bembo's Epitaph on Raphael; A Placid Man's
Epitaph; Epitaph for George Moore

For lines by Gerard Manley Hopkins, to Oxford University Press
on behalf of the Society of Jesus
from *The Poems of Gerard Manley Hopkins* (4th ed. 1967), edited by
W. H. Gardner and N. H. MacKenzie
By Mrs. Hopley; *Of virtues I most warmly bless*

For lines by A. E. Housman, to the Society of Authors as literary
representative of the Estate of A. E. Housman, and Messrs.
Jonathan Cape Ltd.
Here dead we . . . (No. XXXVI); *Some can gaze . . .* (Additional
Poems XVI)

For lines by James Joyce, to the Society of Authors as the literary
    representative of the Estate of James Joyce
    There was a kind Lady called Gregory

For lines by Rudyard Kipling, to the National Trust and Mac-
    millan Company, London and Basingstoke
    from *The Complete Barrack Room Ballads*
    from "Epitaphs of the War":
        A Son; The Coward; The Refined Man; Common Form; A
        Dead Statesman; A Drifter off Tarentum; The Bridegroom

For lines by D. H. Lawrence, to the Estate of the late Mrs. Frieda
    Lawrence and Laurence Pollinger Limited
    from *The Complete Poems of D. H. Lawrence*, Heinemann
        O! Start a Revolution; The Mosquito Knows; Desire is Dead;
        Proper Pride; Food of the North; Lord Tennyson and Lord
        Melchett; "Gross, Coarse, Hideous"; Flowers and Men

For lines by Vachel Lindsay, to Macmillan Publishing Company,
    Inc.
    from *Collected Poems*, Macmillan, © 1914 by Macmillan
    The Leaden-Eyed; What the Moon Saw

For lines by Phyllis McGinley, to the author, Messrs. Secker &
    Warburg Ltd. and the Viking Press, Inc.
    from *The Love Letters of Phyllis McGinley*
    The Old Beauty
    from *Times Three*
        Last Year's Discussion: the Nobel Russian; The Muted
        Screen of Graham Greene; Squeeze Play; The Adversary;
        The Independent; The Demagogue

For lines by Martial, to Mr. James Michie and The Bodley Head
    from *Epigrams of Martial*, Hart Davis, MacGibbon
        i. *Laid with papyrus . . .*; ii. *Whenever you drink all night . . .*;
        iii. *Garland of roses . . .*; iv. *Here, six years old . . .*; v. *Either you
        get out of the house or conform . . .*

For lines by John Masefield, to the Society of Authors as literary
    representative of the Estate of John Masefield, and to
    Macmillan Publishing Company, Inc.
    from *Poems, 1946*, Macmillan, © 1916 by John Masefield
    An Epilogue

For lines by Edgar Lee Masters, to the author and Messrs. Caslsel
   & Collier Macmillan Ltd.
   from *Spoon River Anthology*, Collier Macmillan
      Editor Whedon; Judge Somers; The Circuit Judge

For lines by Adrian Mitchell, to the author and Messrs. Jonathan
   Cape Ltd.
   from *Poems*, Jonathan Cape
      Riddle
   from *The Apeman Cometh*, Jonathan Cape
      Private Transport; Celia Celia

For lines by Marianne Moore, to Messrs. Faber & Faber Ltd. and
   Macmillan Publishing Company, Inc.
   from *The Complete Poems of Marianne Moore*, Faber
   and from *Collected Poems*, Macmillan, © 1935 by Marianne Moore
      Poetry

For lines by J. B. Morton, to Messrs. A. D. Peters & Co. Ltd.
   from *The Best of Beachcomber*, Heinemann
      Epitaph: *A glassblower . . .*; Epitaph: *Tread softly . . .*; *Let poets
      praise the softer winds . . .*

For lines by Ezra Pound, to Messrs. Faber & Faber Ltd. and to New
   Directions Publishing Corporation
   from *Collected Shorter Poems*, Faber
      Translator to Translated; *I dreamt that I was God . . .*; Mr.
      Housman's Message

For lines by Kenneth Rexroth, to Laurence Pollinger Limited
   from *Rexroth Reader*, Jonathan Cape
   and to New Directions Publishing Corporation
   from *Collected Shorter Poems*, © 1956 by New Directions
   from the Persian ("*Naked out of the dark . . .*")

For lines by Edwin Arlington Robinson, to Macmillan Publishing
   Company Inc.
   from *Collected Poems*, Copyright 1915 by Edwin Arlington
   Robinson, renewed 1943 by Ruth Nivison
      The Raven; Doricha; Lais to Aphrodite; An Inscription by
      the Sea

For lines by Theodore Roethke, to Messrs. Faber & Faber Ltd.
   and to Doubleday & Company Inc.

from *The Collected Poems of Theodore Roethke*, Faber
   Academic

For lines by Stevie Smith, to Mr. James MacGibbon, the Executor
   from *The Collected Poems of Stevie Smith*, Allen Lane
       Quand on n'a pas ce que l'on aime . . .; To School!; Dear
       Female Heart; Reversionary; This Englishwoman

For lines by Geoffrey Taylor★
   from *A Dash of Garlick*, privately printed 1932
       Epitaph; English Liberal; Cruel Clever Cat
   from *Withering of the Fig Leaf*, Hogarth, 1927
       Admonition to the Muse
   from *It was not Jones*, "by R. Fitzurse", Hogarth, 1928
       Gentlemen

For lines by Richard Usborne, to the author and Messrs. A. D.
       Peters & Co. Ltd.
       Epitaph on a Party Girl

For lines by Humbert Wolfe, to his daughter, Ann Wolfe
   from *Lampoons*, 1925
       Dean Inge; D. H. Lawrence and James Joyce; Hilaire Belloc
   from *The Uncelestial City*
       The British Journalist

For lines by W. B. Yeats, to Mr. M. B. Yeats, Miss Anne Yeats,
       and the Macmillan Company, London and Basingstoke
   from *The Collected Poems of W. B. Yeats*, Macmillan
       To a Poet, who would have me praise certain bad poets . . .;
       The Coming of Wisdom with Time; To be carved on a Stone
       at Thor Ballylee; Youth and Age; The Nineteenth Century
       and After; Last three lines of *Under Ben Bulben* (*Cast a cold eye*);
       Three Movements

★ While every effort has been made to secure permission, it has in
a few cases proved impossible to trace the author or his executor.
We apologize for our apparent negligence.

Notes and Sources

Sources are mentioned, if known to me, only when they are obscure, or when an epigram is taken from some long work, or is not to be found in the standard edition of the author's poems.

number

1. *The Passetyme of Pleasure*, Tottel's version, 1555.
2. Robbins, *Secular Lyrics of the XIV and XV Centuries*, 1952.
7. Presumably about Thomas Fitzgerald, 10th Earl of Kildare, drawn, hanged and quartered, with his five uncles, at Tyburn, in 1537.
8. Martial, X, 47. *The riches left*: i.e. inherited. *equal friend*: congenial friend. *mean diet*: moderate food.
9. *rechless*: careless, rash.
10. *Greek Anthology*, XI, 418.
11. *Greek Anthology*, VI, 669.
12. *slipper*: slippery. *behight*: promised. *cark*: distress. *affy*: trust.
14. Bodleian, Rawlinson Poet. MS 585. A version of "Amor" in Book ii of *Epigrammata*, by George Buchanan (1506–1582).
17. From three lines of Catullus V.
21. *Letters and Epigrams of Sir John Harrington*. ed. N. E. McClure, Philadelphia, 1930.
22. *Ibid.* Martial, VI, 8.
28. From the gnomic poet Pierre Mathieu (1563–1621).
29. Guy de Pibrac (1529–1584), jurist, long famous for his moralizing *quatraines* on the conduct of life.
32. *Daccus*: Greek δάκος, a biting creature. *gamashes*: gaiters.
35. Frequently printed, and said to come from a tombstone in St. Giles's churchyard, Edinburgh.
36. Frequent in manuscript collections of the 16th–17th centuries.
37. Camden's *Remaines*, 1614 ed.
38. *A Collection of Epigrams*, 1727.
39. *Varia*, ed. Eleanor Brougham, 1925.
40. Grierson, *Poems of John Donne*, 1912.

41. F. Peck, *New Memoirs of the Life and Poetical Works of Mr. John Milton*, 1740. One of several epitaphs formerly ascribed to Shakespeare.

42. Cotgrave, *Wit's Interpreter*, 1655. The Lord Treasurer was Thomas Sackville, Earl of Dorset, who died in 1608.

45. Bastard was parson of Bere Regis, in Dorset.

49–50. Camden's *Remaines*, 1614 ed.

51. *John Hoskyns*, L. B. Osborn, New Haven, 1937.

55. Camden's *Remaines*, 1605 ed.

56. John Aubrey, *Brief Lives*, under Hoskyns.

57. *Greek Anthology*, VII, 348. Camden's *Remaines*, 1605 ed. Title from a Bodleian MS.

58. Camden's *Remaines*, 1605 ed.

59. Sir John Mennis and James Smith, *Musarum Deliciae*, 1655, attached as "The Fart's Epitaph" to a famous piece by several hands, "The Fart censured in the Parliament House", a debate in couplets, member by member:

> But all at last said, it was most fit,
> The Fart as Traitor, to the Tower to commit,
> Whereas they say, it remaines to this hour,
> Yet not close prisoner, but at large in the Tower.

60. This Devil's Christmas pie, Sir Walter Pye (1571–1635), was a Herefordshire neighbour of Serjeant Hoskyns, and like Hoskyns he was a lawyer, Attorney of the Court of Wards.

61. *Reliquiae Wottoniae*, 1651. Sir Albertus Morton (1584?–1625), Secretary of State, half-nephew to Sir Henry Wotton.

62. On the child of Lord Chichester, who was Lord Deputy of Ireland from 1604 to 1614.

67. Étienne Pasquier (1529–1615), jurist and writer. In his Latin epigram the three wives belonged to the Protestant reformer Theodore Beza.

68. John Aubrey, *Brief Lives*. Sir Henry Lee (1530–1597), Master of the Ordnance and Knight of the Garter, an Oxfordshire grandee who lived at Ditchley.

69. *A Collection of Epigrams*, 1727. The lines by George Buchanan (1506–1582) appear in his elegy *Quam misera sit conditio docentium literas humaniores Lutetiae* ("On the wretched condition of teachers of the liberal arts in Paris").

70. Orlando Gibbon's *First Book of Madrigals and Mottets*, 1612. *Greek Anthology*, VI, 1. Lais, the archetypal prostitute of Greek literature.

71. *Witts Recreations,* 1640.

72. H. E. Norfolk, *Gleanings in Churchyards,* 1866. A version of the epitaph on "John Bell Brokenbrow", in Camden's *Remaines,* 1605 ed. Camden says it was at Farlam, in Cumberland. *wame:* belly. *but:* without. *sturt:* quarrelling.

73. Camden's *Remaines,* 1623 ed.

75. Camden's *Remaines,* 1636 ed.

84. L.H., i.e. Lady H. Her identity is unknown.

85. "He lies buryed in the north aisle . . . with this inscription only on him, in a pavement square of blew marble, about 14 inches square . . . which was done at the charge of Jack Young afterwards knighted who, walking there when the grave was covering, gave the fellow eighteen pence to cut it." Aubrey, in *Brief Lives.*
Young belonged to the circle of Suckling and Davenant.

89. Camden's *Remaines,* 1636 ed. Gustavus Adolphus, King of Sweden, was killed in the battle of Lutzen, which his Swedes won, in 1632. The epigram is attributed in MS Ashmole 38 (Bodleian) to Sir Thomas Roe (1581?–1644), the remarkable diplomat, who was admired and rewarded by Gustavus Adolphus. He was friendly with John Donne.

90. Unlikely pieces for a bishop. Corbet was successively Bishop of Oxford and Norwich.

91. Camden's *Remaines,* 1636 ed.

92. Robert Crichton, 6th Lord Sanquhar, hired assassins to kill a fencing master who by accident had put out one of his eyes.

93–97. From *Epigrams Divine and Morall,* 1613, of which only three copies are known. It contains several poems of great charm. The poet was perhaps the Edward May who took his master's degree from Trinity College, Oxford, in 1613, and who seems to have become rector of Crayford in Kent, a Kentish man from West Malling.

94. *ceruse:* cosmetic made of white lead.

97. The original is in John Parkhurst's *Ludicra sive Epigrammata Juvenilia,* 1573. Parkhurst (1512?–1575) was Bishop of Norwich.

101. *Cecubum:* Caecuban wine, one of the best and most desirable Roman wines, mentioned by Martial and Horace. Herrick would have been thinking of Horace's *Eheu, fugaces Postume, Postume* and his 9th epode, in which the pot-boy, the drawer, is instructed to pour out large quantities of Chian, Lesbian and Caecuban wines.

117. Grierson, *The Poems of John Donne,* 1912. Henry Frederick,

Prince of Wales, died, to the general grief, in 1612 when he was 18.

118. *Witts Recreations*, 1640.

119. Camden's *Remaines*, 1636 ed.

120. *Ibid.*

121. In Christ Church, Bristol (Nicholls and Taylor, *Bristol Past and Present*, 1881). Thomas Turner died in 1654.

123. The Countess Dowager of Pembroke was Mary Herbert (1561–1621), 3rd wife of the 2nd Earl, the lusty patroness of poets, including William Browne.

124. *Witts Recreations*, 1640.

125. Cotgrave, *Wit's Interpreter*, 1655.

126. Mennis and Smith, *Musarum Deliciae*, 1656 ed.

127. Cotgrave, *Wit's Interpreter*, 1655.

128–130. From *A Survey of the World in ten Books*, 1661, often charming if sententious distichs.

131. *St. Paul's Church*, 1661.

133. George Villiers, Duke of Buckingham, royal favourite, murdered at Portsmouth in 1628.

135. An epigrammatization of Aristotle's statement (*Poetics*, 17) "Hence poetry comes from genius or madness".

136. *amianthine*: of amianthus, a kind of asbestos. *ignis lambens*: flame which licks or plays without heat.

144. Bodley MS. Rawl. Poet. 66.

145–149. From Watkyns's *Flamma Sine Fumo* (1662), ed. P. C. Davies, Cardiff, 1968. Watkyns was rector of Llanfrynach in Breconshire.

147. Martial, 1, 32.

150. *airth*: point of the compass.

153. Presumably Demokritos, the "Laughing Philosopher".

160. William Prynne (1600–1669), Puritan pamphleteer, and M.P. He was sentenced to be pilloried and branded and have his ears cropped. John Aubrey, *Brief Lives*, records that "His Eares were not quite cutt off, only the upper part, his tippes were visible."

166. Thomas Wentworth, Earl of Strafford, statesman, beheaded in 1641.

167. Abraham Cowley the poet (1618–1667) was a melancholy character and witty Thomas Killigrew (1612–1683) was not the best of playwrights.

168. Martial, V, 58.

170. *Greek Anthology*, XI, 432.

171. *Greek Anthology*, IX, 747. From Stanley's translation of Diogenes Laertius's *History of Philosophy*, 1655–62.

172. *Greek Anthology*, XVI, 210.

173. *Greek Anthology*, V, 83.

174. *Greek Anthology*, IX, 823.

175. From *The Mount of Olives*, 1652. A translation of one of the stanzas of the late 15th century *Englynion y Misoedd* (Stanzas of the Months).

178. Two stories are told of this epigram: one, that Dryden made it up when Kneller had painted Tonson's portrait, the other that he sent it to Tonson when Tonson hadn't paid money owing to him—with a message that there would be more lines to come, if the payment wasn't made.

179. *Penguin Book of Restoration Verse*, ed. H. Love, 1968. Henry Fitzroy, Duke of Grafton, son of Charles II, was hit by a bullet in the storming of Cork in 1690, dying soon after.

180. *A Collection of Epigrams*, 1735 ed.

185. Martial XII, 30.

186. Martial II, 38.

190. Jacques Sirmond (1559–1651), French Jesuit and scholar. Aldrich was Dean of Christ Church, Oxford.

191. In fact the opening lines of "An Historical Poem" (in *The Fourth and Last Collection of Poems, Satyrs, Songs, etc.*, 1689), formerly ascribed to Marvell. They took on a separate existence as an epigram.

192. Auden and Garrett, *The Poet's Tongue*, 1935.

193. The "Poet, whoe'er thou art" was Samuel Pordage (1633–1691?). His tragedy *Heriod and Mariamne* was published in 1673.

195. *A New Collection of Poems and Songs*, 1674.

196. Henry Playford's *Wit and Mirth*, 1684. Set to music by Purcell.

197. *A Collection of Epigrams*, 1727.

198. James Granger's *Biographical History of England*, vol. IV, 1775. Nat Lee, the playwright who collaborated with Dryden, took to drink, and went mad in 1684. He was in Bedlam until 1689.

199. Martial, I, 32. The most familiar version (see also No. 154) of an epigram improved in transmission. It derives from Martial's

> Non amo te, Sabidi, nec possum dicere quare:
> > hoc tantum possum dicere, non amo te
> (I don't love you, Sabidus, I cannot say why:
> > this much I can say, I don't love you)

via Thomas Forde, who in *Faenestra in Pectore* (1660) made Sabidus into "Nell", with the repeated rhyme, and, perhaps, a French version by the Comte Roger de Bussy-Rabatin (1618–1693). Tom Brown, while an undergraduate at Christ Church, Oxford, under the energetic, peremptory dean of the college, John Fell, turned Nell to Fell, and transformed Martial's epigram into what has proved the monument—unfairly—of a great university scholar, builder, and reformer, who was afterwards Bishop of Oxford. In Christ Church cathedral visitors look up at Bishop Fell's memorial stone and remember the epigram; they should also remember that Tom Tower, nearby, was built under Dr. Fell.

200–201. *Amusements Serious and Comical Calculated for the Meridian of London*, 1700.

202. *Mr. T. Brown's Pocket-Book of Common-Places*, in *Works*, 1760.

203. British Library, MS. Harl. 7317.

204. T. Webb, *A New Select Collection of Epitaphs*, 1775. Thomas Fuller (1608–1661), author of *The Worthies*.

205. T. Webb, as above. William Walker (1623–1684). Headmaster of Grantham School, known as "Particles Walker" for his once celebrated *Treatise of English Particles*, 1673.

206. Expansion of a four-line epigram by Georges de Brébeuf (1618–1661).

207. Expansion of a proverb in Erasmus's *Adagiorum collectanea*, 1500.

211. Francis Atterbury (1662–1732). Friend of Pope and his circle, controversialist and champion of clerical independence. Banished for his Jacobite sympathies, 1723.

212. Translated from a Latin epitaph on an earlier litigious Bishop of Rochester, Gilbert de Glanville, who held the see from 1185 to 1214. It was not inscribed on his tomb.

213. Expanded from a six-line epigram by the French poet Jean Ogier de Gombauld (1570–1666). The Latin text opens the chorus in Seneca's play *Thyestes*. The lines were neatly translated by Marvell:

> Climb at court for me that will
> Giddy favour's slippery hill;
> All I seek is to be still.
> Settled in some secret nest,
> In calm leisure let me rest . . .

bottom: skein or ball of thread.

215–216. From two epigrams by the French poet Jacques de Cailly (1604–1675), a favourite with English epigrammatists.

217. Gabriel Gilbert (*c*. 1610–*c*. 1680), French playwright and poet.

218. The epigram by Jean Ogier de Gombauld (1570–1666) on which this was based, was in turn a version of Martial, V, 52.

220. Antoine le Brun (1680–1743).

221. After Plato's epigram, *Greek Anthology* VI, 1, in which the famous prostitute Lais dedicates her mirror to Aphrodite.

222. John Radcliffe (1650–1714), outspoken physician and M.P. The money he left to Oxford University was used to set up the Radcliffe Infirmary, the Radcliffe Observatory and the Radcliffe Library.

223. The sculptor of Prior's bust (on his monument in Westminster Abbey) was the French baroque master Antoine Coysevox (1640–1720).

224. The House of Nassau, to which William of Orange belonged, was traditionally founded in the 11th century. Prior's father was a carpenter at Wimborne, in Dorset.

226. Scévole de Sainte-Marthe (1536–1623), poet and humanist of the circle of Ronsard.

228. *A Collection of Epigrams*, 1727. Tom Hearne (1678–1735), crabbed Oxford scholar and antiquary. "Wormius" in Pope's *Dunciad*.

229. *A Collection of Epigrams*, 1727. Often attributed, wrongly, to Benjamin Franklin.

230. *A Collection of Epigrams*, 1727.

232. Johann von Besser (1654–1729), minor court poet.

234. Bodley MS. Rawl. Poet. 213.

235. *Swift's Miscellanies*. "Colonel" Francis Chartres or Charteris (1675–1732), soldier, landowner, cheat, gambler, and thief, was found guilty of rape in 1730, but pardoned.

236. *A Collection of Epigrams*, 1727.

240. Attached to Swift's "Elegy on the Supposed Death of Partridge the Almanack-Maker". Swift in 1704 published a satirical prediction that Partridge would die on 29 March 1708. Then on 30 March 1708 he published a description of his death, as foretold. Partridge had difficulty in persuading the public he was still alive.

242. Rebecca Dingley was the friend and companion of Esther Johnson, Swift's Stella.

246. Written by Swift to be inscribed, in deep letters, strongly gilded, on his tombstone in St. Patrick's Cathedral, Dublin.

247–249. *Poems*, Dublin 1742.

250–251. Nichols, *Literary Anecdotes*, iii, 330. Trapp (1679–1747) was Oxford's first Professor of Poetry. George I bought the celebrated library of John Moore, Bishop of Ely, and gave it to Cambridge University, at the time of the Jacobite risings, when Oxford's loyalty was suspect.

252. See note above. The first volume of Trapp's *Aeneid* appeared in 1718.

253. Evans had in mind Blenheim Palace, designed by Sir John Vanbrugh (1664–1726).

254. Amhurst's *Terrae-Filius* No. XX, 1721. Evans published his long poem *The Apparition: A Dialogue betwixt the Devil and a Doctor concerning the rights of the Christian Church*, in 1710.

255. Appears in many 18th century collections. Abel Evans was chaplain of St. John's College, Oxford.

259. A parody of the brief eulogistic epitaph on the tomb of Pico della Mirandola, in San Marco, Florence. Lord Coningsby (1656?–1729), Whig politician, litigious and sharp, was suspected of corruption and self enrichment. He moved the impeachment in 1717 of Harley, the Tory statesman, and friend of Pope and Swift.

261. James Moore Smythe (1702–1734), born James Moore, took the name Smythe on inheriting his grandfather's fortune. For this coxcomb and spendthrift, see Pope's *Dunciad*.

Ex nihilo nihil fit: nothing is born of nothing.

265. Colley Cibber (1671–1757), playwright and poet, and Lewis Theobald (1688–1744), editor of Shakespeare, were both victimized by Pope in *The Dunciad*. They were both in the running for the Laureateship, which went to Cibber (1730). Stephen Duck (1705–1756), farm labourer and poet from Wiltshire, was ordained, and patronized by George II's Queen Caroline.

268. The critic John Dennis (1657–1734).

269. Cf. No. 242 by Swift.

270. Robert Freind (1667–1751), Headmaster of Westminster School, was in demand for monumental inscriptions in Latin.

271. Not certainly by Pope, though it seems in his manner. See Pope, *Minor Poems*, ed. Ault and Butt.

274. The Shakespeare monument and statue in the Abbey (1740) were paid for by public subscription. Pope, Lord Burlington and

Dr. Richard Mead administered the funds, and gave the commission to the sculptor, Peter Scheemakers.

279. Made up on horseback by Pope and Parnell.

280. Lord Lyttelton's poem *Advice to a Lady* appeared in 1733.

282. The more decorous epitaph which Pope wrote on the doom by lightning of John Hewet (not Hughes) and Sarah Drew can still be seen affixed to the south wall of Stanton Harcourt church, Oxfordshire.

283. *A Collection of Epigrams*, 1735. From an anonymous epigram in the *Greek Anthology* (XVI, 168) on the Aphrodite of Knidos, itself a variant of an epigram by Plato.

284. *A Collection of Epigrams*, 1727.

285. *A Collection of Epigrams*, 1727. Annibal Cruceius (1509–1577), Milanese poet, based his epigram on Martial XI, 71. John Woodward (1665–1728), London physician and geologist.

286. *The British Martial*, 1806.

287. Booth, *Epigrams Ancient and Modern*, 1863. After a Latin epigram by the great French poet du Bellay (1522–1560). For Johnson's version see No. 303.

288. Nicholas Amhurst's *Terrae-Filius*, No. XX, 1721.

289. In many 18th-century collections. In 1756 the Worcester physician John Wall published an analysis of the healing waters of St. Ann's Well, Malvern. He declared Malvern water was made efficacious by its "great purity and absence of mineral matter".

290. The monopolists Joseph Yates and William Dawson, "two tall meagre men", leased the Manchester mills on which Manchester Grammar School depended. The legal compulsion to grind corn and malt at these mills and nowhere else in Manchester become more and more irksome as the town increased. The monopoly of the corn mill was abolished in 1758 by act of parliament.

291. Giovanni Batista Bononcini (1670–1747), operatic composer, was brought to London in 1720 by the anti-Hanoverians, to offset Handel who was the court favourite.

To "tweedle" is to strum on a musical instrument; a tweedle-dee is a high note strummer, a tweedle-dum a low note strummer.

292. Byrom (see No. 291) was anti-Hanoverian and favoured the Pretender.

293. H. J. Loaring, *Curious Records*, 1872.

294–295. *Works of Hildebrand Jacob*, 1735.

296. Sir Thomas Robinson (1700?–1777), of Rokeby, M.P., architect and dilettante, a long thin man known for his long speeches and his pretentiousness, was distinguished as "long Sir Thomas", from his squat namesake Sir Thomas Robinson, a diplomat.

300. Booth, *Epigrams Ancient and Modern*, 1863.

301. Isaac de Benserade (1612–1691), writer of masques, elegies, epigrams, who translated Ovid's *Metamorphoses* into rondeaux.

303. See No. 287, and note.

304. Thomas Warton (1728–1790), Professor of Poetry at Oxford, poet laureate, author of the first *History of English Poetry*. See No. 331.

305. Extempore version of an Italian epigram on Francis III who fled from his duchy of Modena because of a comet which appeared in 1742, when Modena was threatened by the troops of the King of Sardinia.

307. William Whitehead became poet laureate in 1757.

308. C. S. Carey, *A Commonplace Book of Epigrams*, 1872.

309. Printed in many collections. Alexis Piron (1689–1773) French poet, epigrammatist and dramatist. Louis XV was induced to veto his election to the Académie Française in 1753 because he had once written an indecent "Ode to Priapus".

310. Ascribed to Shenstone in T. Webb's *New Select Collection of Epitaphs*, 1775.

311–313. Edmund Keene (1714–1781) was a Fellow and later Master of Peterhouse, Cambridge (Gray's college), then Bishop of Ely, and of Chester. According to William Cole (quoted in the *Dictionary of National Biography*) he was "as much puffed up with his dignities and fortune as any on the bench."

314. On the Rev. Henry Etough, a dissenter ordained an Anglican priest. Gray's friend William Cole (see *Poems of Gray, Collins and Goldsmith*, ed. Lonsdale, 1969) described him as "a pimping tale-bearing dissenting teacher, who by adulation and flattery, and an everlasting fund of news and scandal, made himself agreeable to many of prime fortune . . . at Cambridge . . . a busy impertinent meddler in everyone's affairs."

  Tophet: i.e. "Etough" re-ordered. (See *Jeremiah* 19.4 and *Paradise Lost* 1. 404).

317. Sterne died in 1768.

318. "Sir" John Hill (1716–1775) was both quack doctor and writer.

321. Booth, *Epigrams Ancient and Modern*, 1863.

322. *Ibid.*

323. H. J. Loaring, *Curious Records*, 1872. Said to have been from a Sussex gravestone.

326. Nuneham Park, Nuneham Courtney, Oxfordshire, the home of Walpole's friend, Simon Harcourt.

327. The translator was the much ridiculed Edward Burnaby Greene, a wealthy brewer, whose *Works of Anacreon and Sappho* was published in 1768.

330. Mark Lemon, *The Jest Book*, 1864. Henry Harington (1727–1816) was a Bath doctor and musician.

331. Martial, *De Spectaculis*, 25 B. On Warton's stuffed style, see No. 304.

332–333. From *Retaliation*, Goldsmith's sequence of epitaphs. Tommy Townshend (1733–1800), Home Secretary, etc. (He became Lord Sydney.)

335. *Greek Anthology*, VII, 348. T. Webb, *A New Select Collection of Epitaphs*, 1775. See also No. 57.

336. T. Webb, *New Select Collection of Epitaphs*, 1775.

338. *Frobisher's New Select Collection of Epitaphs* (*c.* 1791).

339. Bodley MS. Top. gen. e.52. From St. Dunstan's churchyard, Stepney.

340. Bodley MS. Eng. poet c.51. From Bedwell churchyard, Herts.

341. From *Epigrammata*, Lib. III, CXCV, by the famous John Owen (1560?–1622).

342. *Greek Anthology*, VII, 307, by the Byzantine poet Paulos, 6th century AD. Cf. No. 457.

343. The Persian quatrain of which this is a close translation, will be found in Claud Field's *Dictionary of Oriental Quotations*, 1911.

344. Thomas Moore's celebrated but very artificial *Odes of Anacreon* appeared in 1800, his first book.

345. J. A. Lovat Fraser, *Erskine*, 1932. Sir James Alan Park (1703–1838), justice of the common pleas. Known for his bad temper.

346. Two lines, which became repeated as an epigram, from Sheridan's long poem *Clio's Protest*, 1771.

347. Lady Anne Hamilton (1766–1846), eldest daughter of the Duke of Hamilton, remembered for her intimate friendship with Queen Caroline, the notorious wife of George IV.

348. John Nichols, *A Select Collection of Poems*, Vol. 6, 1782.

349. *Facetiae Cantabrigienses*, by "Socius", 1825– in which it is explained that Mansel, at Cambridge (when he became Master of Trinity) added to the two opening lines of a poem he found on

another undergraduate's table.

350. Presumably by Rowlandson or one of his friends, and inscribed on a churchyard tomb in his print "Meditation among the Tombs". Whoever wrote it was aware that *vagina* is the Latin for scabbard.

355. R. H. Cromek (1770–1812), engraver and publisher; Thomas Stothard (1755–1834), neo-classic artist.

356. See above.

357–358. William Hayley, insipid but well-to-do poet (1745–1820), who patronized Blake.

361. William Flaxman (1755–1826), neo-classic sculptor and draughtsman.

369. *Troutbeck.* By a Member of the Scandinavian Society, 1876. Presumably by the artist and humorist Julius Caesar Ibbetson. He painted the quatrain on his signboard for the Mortal Man inn at Troutback, in the Lakes, together with two speakers, one fat and red-nosed, one thin and pallid.

370. *Facetiae Cantabrigienses*, by "Socius", 1825. Porson's version of an epigram in Greek by an Etonian, which was based on epigrams by Demodokos (*Greek Anthology*, XI, 236) and Phokylides (Edmonds, *Elegy and Iambus*, 1931). Johann Gottfried Jakob Hermann (1772–1848) was classical scholar, editor and philologist.

371. J. S. Watson, *Life of Richard Porson*, 1861.

372. *Facetiae Cantabrigienses*, by "Socius", 1825. Porson claimed that he could pun on any subject, and was challenged to pun on the Latin gerunds, with this result (which was suggested by one of John Owen's epigrams (*Epigrammata*, VIII, XXXI, "*Di-do, dum Aeneas aberat ...*").

373. Booth, *Epigrams Ancient and Modern*, 1863.

374. *Facetiae Cantabrigienses*, by "Socius", 1825. Comic effect or no, Brunck and Ruhnken of course existed, two of the greatest of European classicists, R. F. P. Brunck (1729–1803) of Strasbourg, editor of the *Greek Anthology*, Anakreon, Sophokles, etc., and David Ruhnken (1723–1798) of the University of Leiden, a sociable, free-living scholar of Greek and Latin.

375. J. S. Watson, *Life of Richard Porson*, 1861.

380. *fient a bit*: devil a bit, none at all, damn all.

381. John Stewart, 7th Earl of Galloway (1736–1806), contemner of Burns.

387. Mr. E——, i.e. James Elphinston (1721–1809). Dr. Johnson

remarked of his Martial translations (1782) that they had in them "too much folly for madness" and "too much madness for folly".

390. H. J. Loaring, *Curious Records*, 1872. Sir Nathaniel Wraxall (1751–1831) wrote *Historical Memoirs of my own Time*, 1815.

391. On an ornamental stone urn which till recent years stood lost among bushes in the ruined garden at Hafod, in Cardiganshire. Rogers wrote the epitaph, on the death of her pet robin, for the daughter of Thomas Johnes, the rich scholarly proprietor of Hafod.

392. *Table-Talk of Samuel Rogers*, 1856. John William Ward (1781–1833), Tory M.P., and afterwards the 1st Earl of Dudley.

393. W. D. Adams, *English Epigrams*, n.d.

394. *Table-Talk of Samuel Rogers*, 1856.

395. *Frobisher's New Select Collection of Epitaphs* (*c.* 1791).

396. From *The Anti-Jacobin*. Usually ascribed to George Canning, though it seems to have been a joint effort by several contributors. It was a satirical anti-revolutionary parody of Southey's "IN-SCRIPTION *for the Apartment in Chepstow Castle, where Henry Marten, the Regicide, was imprisoned thirty years.*" Elizabeth Brownrigg, midwife, was hanged at Tyburn in 1767 for murdering, in fact, one of her three apprentices.

397. B. Burnett, *Reply to the Report of the Commissioners of Enquiry at the Cape of Good Hope upon the Complaints Addressed to the Colonial Government*, London, 1826. Willem Stephanus van Rÿneveld (1765–1812), President of the Court of Justice. He killed himself. The Government Gazette on his death: "Merit so various and alike conspicuous will ever remain the boast and pride of the Cape of Good Hope." The Dutch despised him as a toady to the British.

Quinbus Flestrin: Gulliver, the man-mountain according to the Lilliputians, in *Gulliver's Travels*.

398. From *Peveril of the Peak*.

399. From *Old Mortality*.

400. Scott's *Journal*, Dec. 18, 1826.

401. Scott's *Journal*. Scott left Mrs. Brown's lodgings in North St. David Street, Edinburgh, on July 13, 1826.

402. Attributed to Sydney Smith. He denied it (John Timbs, *A Century of Anecdote*, 1864, quoted in Dodd, *The Epigrammatists*, 1875), but it is certainly in his manner of wit and statement. Charles Blomfield (1786–1857), Bishop of London, issued a charge to his clergy in 1842, against the Tractarians.

403. Francis Jeffrey (1773–1850), lawyer, and editor of *The Edin-*

burgh Review. A Whig, and a Reform Bill man, like Sydney Smith.

404. J. O. Lettsom (1744–1815), eminent Quaker physician in London.

405. A. J. Loaring, *Curious Records*, 1872.

407. Cf. "the dwarfish poetry" in Sedley's epigram. No. 189.

425. For the Georges, see also Nos. 460 and 504.

426. Statue (1834) by Sir Richard Westmacott topping the column on Carlton House Tower, London.

428. William Gifford (1756–1826). Editor of the *Quarterly Review*: the savage reviewer of Keats.

430. Did Landor make up the quotation from Moore? The nearest I can find in Moore's poems is

> Whether thou lyest on springing flowers
> Drunk with the balmy morning-showers

translated from Rapin. (Moore's *Odes of Anacreon*, note to Ode XXIV).

453. Sir Isaac Heard (1730–1822), Garter King-of-Arms.

454. Lord Castlereagh, Foreign Secretary from 1812 to 1822.

455. Lord Roden (1731–1797), Irish peer, who supported Protestant religious societies and was Grand Master of the Orange Order.

456. Southey became Poet Laureate in 1813.

457. *Greek Anthology*, VII, 307. Cf. Cowper's version, No. 342.

458. *Diary and Correspondence of Lord Colchester*, 1861 (Diary Nov. 15, c. 1820.). George IV's queen (1768–1821).

459. *Dictionary of National Biography*, XIV, 1115. The 2nd Earl of Onslow (1755–1827), M.P. and eccentric.

460. Horace Walpole, *Memoirs of the Last Ten Years of the Reign of George II, 1822*. Frederick Augustus, Duke of York (1763–1827), 2nd son of George III.

461. H. J. Loaring, *Curious Records*, 1872.

462. From *Punch*. Edward Jenner (1749–1823), discoverer of vaccination for smallpox.

469. See note on No. 454.

472. Byron wrote this in 1820 about his wife Anne Isabella Milbanke. They married in 1815 and separated in 1816.

474. *Eheu* ... Horace, *Odes* II, XIV: Alas the swift years glide away, Posthumus, Postumus. *O mihi praeteritos* ... Virgil *Aeneid*, VIII, 560: O if Jupiter would give me back the lost years.

475. Townsend was the witty rector of Kingston-by-Sea, Sussex,

where a tablet in the church records his friendship with "the literary patrons of his time".

477. *Greek Anthology*, VII, 249.

479. Mark Lemon, *The Jest Book*, 1864. John Scott, Earl of Eldon (1751–1838), Lord Chief Justice and eventually Lord Chancellor. Sir Charles Weatherell (1770–1846), reactionary and unpopular politician and chancery lawyer.

480. Quoted by Tom Moore in a note to his "Epistle from Henry of Exeter to John of Tuam"—i.e. to the dictatorial Archbishop of Tuam, Power le Poer Trench (1770–1839).

481. Aubrey Stewart, *English Epigrams and Epitaphs*, 1897. The Legion of Honour was founded by Napoleon in 1802. According to Brewer's *Dictionary of Phrase and Fable* by 1843 there were 49,417 members.

483. Dedication to Hood's *Whims and Oddities*, 1826.

486. Donald and Catherine Carswell, *The Scots Week-End*, 1936.

488. Eleanor Brougham, *Varia*, 1925.

490. Kennedy, Headmaster of Shrewsbury School, was the author of the famous *Latin Primer*.

491. Booth, *Epigrams Ancient and Modern*, 1863.

492. H. E. Norfolk, *Gleanings in Graveyards*, 1886.

493. *Legends, Tales and Songs in the Dialect of the Peasantry of Gloucestershire* n.d.

494. *Notes and Queries*, 1889.

495. Quoted by William Barnes in "Thoughts on Beauty and Art", *Macmillan's Magazine*, IV, 1861.

496. W. D. Adams, *English Epigrams*. Alexis Soyer (1809–1858), the great chef of the Reform Club, London, who worked with Florence Nightingale in the Crimea. For the story of the voice which said "The great god Pan is dead", see Plutarch's dialogue *De defectu oraculorum* (tr. Rex Warner, *Plutarch: Moral Essays*, Penguin, 1971). Soyer was also famous for *The Pantropheon* (1853), a history of food.

498. Christopher North (John Wilson) reviewed Tennyson's *Poems, Chiefly Lyrical* in *Blackwood's Magazine*, May 1832.

502. Bertrand Payne managed the publishing firm of Edward Moxon.

504. First published in *Punch*, in its radical days. See 425 and 460.

505. H. J. Daniel, grocer and poet, of Lostwithiel, in Cornwall.

510. H. J. Loaring, *Curious Records*, 1872.

511. *Ibid.*; in a slightly different version.

512. *Ibid.*; from the churchyard of Upton-on-Severn.

514. Booth, *Epigrams Ancient and Modern*, 1863.

515. H. J. Loaring, *Curious Records*, 1872. From Edinburgh churchyard.

516. *Ibid.*; said to have been in Lambeth churchyard.

517. Eleanor Brougham, *Varia*, 1925.

525. Champney, *Memoirs and Correspondence of Coventry Patmore*, 1900. I, 286. Written after the report in the *Times*, August 8, 1870.

526. From a French epigram of earlier date (*Notes and Queries* 4th series, VII, 34) quoted by Napoleon's General Dumas in his *Précis des événements militaires*.

528–532. Thorold Rogers, *Epistles, Satires and Epigrams*, 1876.

533. W. H. Hutton, *Letters of Bishop Stubbs*, 1904.

534. *Ibid.*, from a letter to J. R. Green, Dec. 17, 1871. Kingsley was Cambridge's unhistorical Professor of History, 1860–1869, and his friend James Anthony Froude delivered an anti-clerical address to the students of St. Andrews as their Rector, 1868.

535. Dorothea Beale (1831–1906) and Frances Mary Buss (1827–1894), pioneers of education for women, Principal and Vice-Principal of the Ladies' College, Cheltenham.

536. The *Balliol Rhymes* were first circulated round Oxford University in a broadsheet.

   i. Benjamin Jowett, Master of Balliol College, 1870–1893.

   ii. J. W. Mackail (1854–1945). Scholar, biographer of William Morris, translator from the *Greek Anthology* (in prose), and Oxford's Professor of Poetry.

   iii. Solomon Lee (1859–1926). Later Sir Sidney Lee, editor of the *Dictionary of National Biography*.

   iv. G. N. Curzon (1958–1925). Later Marquess Curzon of Kedleston, Viceroy of India, and Foreign Secretary.

   vii. Sir William Anson (1843–1914), made Warden of All Souls, 1881.

   viii. H. G. Liddell (1811–1898), the Liddell of Liddell and Scott's *Greek Lexicon*.

537–538. Valentine Prinsep (1838–1904). Royal Academician, 1894. His best pictures were realistic modern subjects influenced by the Pre-Raphaelites.

540. Sir William Agnew (1825–1910) and Thomas Agnew (1827–1883), London dealers in art, especially in old masters.

541. Ernest Gambart (1814–1902), Belgian born art dealer, son of

a fraudulent businessman. He made a fortune out of popular artists including Frith, Rosa Bonheur and Alma Tadema.

553. *Greek Anthology*, VII, 80. On the poet Herakleitos of Halikarnassos. *Nightingales*, the title of a book of his poems.

557–558. John Milton Hay was U.S. Ambassador to London 1897–1898, and Secretary of State. No. 558 is a translation of Heine's "Das Glück ist eine leichte Dirne."

560. *Greek Anthology*, VII, 309, by an unknown poet on Dionysos of Tarsos; but Hardy made his epigram from a French version of the Greek.

562. Part of the Latin epitaph which the humanist Pietro Bembo (1470–1547) wrote for his friend Raphael's tombstone in the Pantheon in Rome.

565. "Mrs. Hopley": apparently a family name—from Hop(kins) and (Man)ley, for Hopkins' mother.

568. *Greek Anthology*, XI, 186.

569. Gow and Page, *Hellenistic Epigrams*, 17 (2nd century BC).

570. *Greek Anthology*, VI, 1.

571. *Greek Anthology*, VIII, 285.

574. Like the epigram on Doctor Fell (No. 199), these famous lines are of mixed ancestry, and have improved in transmission. They were spoken by J. C. Bossidy as a toast, beginning "And this is the good old Boston", at the Holy Cross Alumni dinner in 1910. Bossidy had adapted them from a toast given some years before at the 25th anniversary dinner of the Harvard Class of 1880.

582. The last 3 lines of Yeats's *Under Bell Bulben*, VI.

584. Auden, *Oxford Book of Light Verse*, 1938.

593. *Avril*, 1945 (an inferior version in Belloc's *Complete Verse*, 1970). François de Malherbe (1885–1628), poetical reformer in the early period of French *classicisme*.

631. *54 Conceits*, 1933.

632. Gogarty, *As I was going down Sackville Street*, 1937.

646. Lord Melchett (1868–1930), formerly Sir Alfred Mond, industrialist and financier, did not endear himself to authors by buying and degrading *The English Review*, to which Lawrence and others of the new century had contributed, under the editorship of Ford Madox Ford. The first two lines are from Tennyson's "The Northern Farmer: New Style."

649. William Ralph Inge (1860–1954), trenchant journalizing Dean of St. Paul's from 1911 to 1934.

654. A translation of the first stanza of Heine's "Mir träumt' ich bin der liebe Gott."

657. *Greek Anthology*, XVI, 153.

658. *Ibid.*, VII, 532.

659. *Ibid.*, IX, 44.

660. *Ibid.*, VI, 228.

663. *The Times*, January 22, 1975. She was a Hungarian-born Marxist imprisoned by the Hungarian communists for seven years, an experience she described in *Seven Years Solitary*, 1957.

666–670. *Mournful Numbers*, 1932.

671–673. *The Best of Beachcomber.*

687. *On English Poetry*, 1922.

690. *Greek Anthology*, VII, 211.

691. *A Dash of Garlic*, by G.T. (privately printed, 1933).

692. *Ibid.*

693. *Withering of the Fig Leaf*, 1927.

694. See note above on 691.

695. *It Was Not Jones*, by R. Fitzurse (i.e. Geoffrey Taylor), 1928.

704. N. Rosten, *The Big Road*, 1945. Written up in a U.S. army latrine, in the Second World War.

705. From an English public lavatory.

723. From Martial, X, 97; XII, 12: IX, 60; X, 74; XI, 104.

Index of Writers

Index of First Lines

273

277

283